YEAH, BUT...

CUT THROUGH THE NOISE TO LIVE, LEARN, AND LEAD BETTER

MARC A. WOLFE

First published in 2025, Nashville, Tennessee, USA
© 2025, Logic Catalyst Press
Yeah, But… Cut Through The Noise To Live, Learn, And Lead Better,
Marc A. Wolfe

Logic Catalyst Press

Library of Congress Control Number: 2024925808

ISBN Paperback [979-8-9908182-0-0]
ISBN Hardback [979-8-9908182-1-7]
ISBN Ebook [979-8-9908182-3-1]
ISBN Audiobook [979-8-9908182-2-4]

All rights reserved. No part of this book may be reproduced, scanned, stored in a retrieval system, or distributed in any form including printed or electronic without prior written permission from the author. Please do not participate in or encourage piracy of copyrighted materials.

Created in conjunction with The Book Shelf:
Editor: Shaun Hand
Typesetter: Kyle Albuquerque
Cover designer: Niall Burgess
Proofreader: Gemma Rowlands

Although the author has made every effort to ensure that the information in this book was correct at the time of publishing, and while this publication is designed to provide accurate information on the subject matter covered, the author assumes no responsibility for errors, inaccuracies, omissions, or any other inconsistencies herein, and hereby disclaims any liability to any party for any loss, damage, or disruption caused by errors or omissions, whether such errors or omissions result from negligence, accident, or any other cause. The author makes no guarantees concerning the level of success you may experience by following the advice contained in this book, and you accept the risk that results will differ for each individual.

Trademarks mentioned are owned by their respective companies and our use does not imply endorsement or recommendation.

https://www.marcAwolfe.com

TABLE OF CONTENTS

DEDICATION	5
EPIGRAPH	7
INTRODUCTION	9
CHAPTER 1: YEAH, BUT… I'M NOT READY	17
CHAPTER 2: YEAH, BUT… SOMEBODY ALREADY DID IT	27
CHAPTER 3: YEAH, BUT… I DON'T HAVE TIME	37
CLIENT CASE STUDY: DON BAHAM–SMALL STEPS IN THE RIGHT DIRECTION	45
CHAPTER 4: YEAH, BUT… I DON'T KNOW WHERE TO START	51
CHAPTER 5: YEAH, BUT… I DON'T KNOW WHAT TO DO NEXT	61
CHAPTER 6: YEAH, BUT… WHAT'S THE PLAN?	71
CLIENT CASE STUDY: KEVIN DOSTALER AND THE VALUE OF KNOWING WHEN TO BE LED	81
CHAPTER 7: YEAH, BUT… I'M NOT SURE I CAN DO IT	85
CHAPTER 8: YEAH, BUT… IT'S NOT SAFE	95
CHAPTER 9: YEAH, BUT… I NEED HELP!	105

COLLEAGUE CASE STUDY:
MARC DEDMAN–NAVIGATING YOUR OWN YEAH, BUTS
AND THOSE OF OTHERS   117

CHAPTER 10: YEAH, BUT… I'M TOO OLD OR TOO YOUNG   121

CHAPTER 11: YEAH, BUT… YOU CAN'T WHERE I
COME FROM   131

CHAPTER 12: YEAH, BUT… I'M NOT QUALIFIED   141

CLIENT CASE STUDY:
GABRIELLE THOMPSON–THE YEAH, BUTS OF AN
INSPIRATIONAL YOUNG LEADER   151

CHAPTER 13: YEAH, BUT… I DON'T FEEL SUCCESSFUL   155

CHAPTER 14: YEAH, BUT… WHAT WILL OTHERS SAY
OR THINK?   165

CHAPTER 15: YEAH, BUT… WHAT IF I FAIL?   175

CHAPTER 16: YEAH, BUT… NOW WHAT?   185

WHAT'S NEXT?   189

ACKNOWLEDGMENTS   191

ABOUT THE AUTHOR   193

REFERENCES   195

DEDICATION

To Laura, my forever bride by my side, in our unified pursuit of the Lord's plan for me, our life, and our family.

To Brooks and Brenna, our dynamic duo daughters.

In memory of Katherine M. Wolfe, my mom, who was always an advocate and gave selflessly to make sure everything was, as she would say, "peachy creamy."

EPIGRAPH

"Nothing is more common than unfulfilled potential."

- Howard Hendricks

INTRODUCTION

I want you to be completely honest, both with me and yourself. How many times have you had a dream, goal, or aspiration in life that you gave up on? Maybe even quit before you started trying? How many times have you felt stuck in your work or personal life? And how many times have you wished that life was different—that life was better?

I'm willing to bet that you ran out of fingers to count on. Because here's the thing, most of us want more from life and have countless dreams of how life could be better, but at the same time, we also think that *this is all there is*. This is all we're capable of. This is all we can do or be.

We don't see that what we value and dream of is possible, let alone probable. As a result, our potential remains unfulfilled, and we don't move forward as much as we could. We start projects only to abandon them without achieving what we intended, and we wind up feeling stuck, whether it's in our career or our personal life. On the surface, it might look to others like we're living the dream, but we know deep down that we're not. We want more from life. It's something we believe ourselves capable of but find near impossible to attain.

There are reasons why this happens. Sometimes, there are real-world obstacles or limitations in our way. Other times, the restrictions are self-imposed and actually only exist in our minds. Real or imagined, they can be equally frustrating, holding us back from being who we were made to be and from doing what we know we should be doing. They make us undervalue our gifts and undersell our strengths.

All too often, we respond to not achieving our dreams (or not trying to achieve them) by coming up with excuses that begin, "Yeah, but…" This book is about those excuses. It's about those phrases that often reveal a lack of self-confidence; that focus only on the obstacles that, generally speaking, are only in our heads.

Maybe you instantly recognize some of these phrases, like "Yeah, but… I don't have the time," or "Yeah, but… I'm too old." We all have the same or similar thoughts. We all make excuses for not doing the things we wish we could do. But if you constantly let your Yeah, Buts define you and hold you back, then time and the world won't wait for you to get it together. You'll stay stuck. Your wish that life would somehow be different will remain just that: a wish.

Those two small, monosyllabic words *yeah* and *but* are something we use as a weapon against ourselves. They stop us from becoming who we want to be, should be, were made to be, and can be. I know this because I've heard Yeah, Buts my whole life. When I started my first business as a freelance photographer at 16 years old, I captured moments in time with everyone from professional football teams to national politicians. Later, I founded a company that supported worldwide organizations with their Apple computers. And in those seemingly very different places, I noticed the same thing: people got so caught up in *what* they were doing that they forgot *why* they'd started doing it in the first place.

So, I started asking them a question. It wasn't about what they were doing or what they did at their job; it was, "What do you want to become?"

A surprising amount had no idea, but an even more surprising amount could elaborate on what they wanted to become, often in great detail, yet still had no strategy for making it happen. But whichever way they answered, when I tried to delve deeper, they always gave me… you guessed it, "Yeah, but…"

INTRODUCTION

I saw it again and again:

The CEO who was too busy working 70+ hours a week to remember work-life balance or, as I like to call it life agility[1] and recall what their purpose was.

The leader who felt overwhelmed by their career and wanted to add meaning to their life and leave a legacy, not just a career history on LinkedIn.

The executive who'd worked their way up to a leadership position but felt they were more than just their job and wanted to create, build, or design something different.

These were elite professionals. They had reached coveted leadership roles but were still struggling to get it right. They had a desire to help and support others, but it was diluted and barely a glimmer of what it once was. With every passing birthday, they felt the discomfort of dreams they'd given up on, and they felt stuck with an increasing burden of responsibility and an all-consuming career.

Yet they also had an endless supply of Yeah, Buts to stop them from doing something different. Ultimately, they felt that it wasn't possible to start something new. They didn't feel it was realistic, so they'd given up and accepted it: "This is who I am. I work. I earn. I am a spouse. I am a parent. This is how life is and how it will remain. That was a dream for a different me; that time has come and gone."

But the more I heard the same scenarios and excuses being rolled out, the more certain I knew that it didn't have to be this way. At the time, my role was to support and advise different leaders—corporate executives, company principals, division directors, etc.— through technological challenges and show them new ways to think about specific problems, but I increasingly saw the parallels between that and overcoming personal barriers. Both involved appraising the current situation, seeing what was possible, and incrementally moving forward from there. Although I didn't know it at the time, that realization was the genesis of this book.

There were further signposts too, such as the recognition that experience and knowledge are invaluable but those resources need to meet the wisdom of knowing what to do and when.

That's why this book is here. It's a resource to empower you with that wisdom providing you with opportunities for getting unstuck, banishing your Yeah, Buts, and moving forward so you can live, learn, and lead better—maybe even start something new.

Whatever your dream, you'll discover how to work through any real or imagined limitations that are holding you back. And if the obstacles are real, you can see whether you can work through them or walk around them. And you'll start gaining traction through your actions, meaning you'll see that *it is possible*. It's not too late.

The good news is that when you start to see how things *can* be, it creates acceleration, and that acceleration is momentum. And momentum gets you to a place where it's hard to stop. That vital tipping point is where this book will take you.

Just for a moment, imagine what it would feel like to be able to pursue your dreams and aspirations, the ones you left behind or gave up on. I know it's tough to get there, and that's why I'll give you clear steps to understand what it looks and feels like to accomplish a pursuit and take actions that move you beyond your current position in life. You'll see simple ways that people have overcome the Yeah, But you're facing, from leaders to celebrities and people you've never heard of.

I'll also show you that sometimes, a Yeah, But is simply a flaw in our thinking, such as looking at something from the perspective of failure, and I'll show you the proven ways to get over it.

Each chapter covers a different Yeah, But. You don't have to read it from cover to cover; simply pick out those examples you recognize from that little voice in your head. If you want to read it in order though, that's also fine, especially if you hear yourself coming up with varied excuses for not seeing things through. You'll also find a "Yeah, But Quickfinder" that groups similar Yeah, Buts together.

In this book, you'll also read case studies of historical figures, household names, and just a few of the many executives I've helped. All faced their Yeah, Buts and overcame them. You'll also see how most people, from all walks of life, have multiple Yeah, Buts that keep them stuck. They're people just like you, and they persevered to move from Yeah, But to unstuck.

But I'm going to be candid with you, too. I'm here to challenge you, not praise or criticize what you're not doing. I'm also not here to debunk your Yeah, Buts with facts and statistics. There's plenty of that stuff out there already, and I don't think it works. I'm here to provide a different angle and get you to see things from your own different perspective too. I'm not here to shame or embarrass you into thinking differently, either. I'm here to reframe the world so you can paint the picture that goes inside it.

I also want to put in a major caveat before we start. There is no shame in feeling stuck, being afraid, or struggling with your mental health. It's unfortunate that the corporate world is too often unable to acknowledge that people struggle. However, I am a professional consultant and executive coach, not a psychologist or therapist, so I cannot diagnose or advise on those things or offer analysis on why they happened. I'm here to offer practical ways to kick your Yeah, Buts in the butt by *deciding* and then *acting*. If you need further support, please consult a relevant qualified professional.

It's time to stop letting obstacles sit like never-ending road construction in your head, holding everything up and wasting your precious time on the journey of life. When you move past your Yeah, Buts, you can envision and build. You can dream big and start creating a living legacy. You can thrive in your career *and* be more than your profession. And you can do and be so much more than you currently believe yourself capable of.

So let's get started, although just by reading this, you already have. It's time to turn your Yeah, Buts around!

YEAH, BUT QUICKFINDER
Find the path to quickly bust your Yeah, But…

TIME-BASED BUTS

Chapter 1: I'm Not Ready	17
Chapter 2: Somebody Already Did It	27
Chapter 3: I Don't Have Time	37

PATH-BASED BUTS

Chapter 4: I Don't Know Where to Start	51
Chapter 5: I Don't Know What to Do Next	61
Chapter 6: What's The Plan?	71

WORRY-BASED BUTS

Chapter 7: I'm Not Sure I Can Do It	85
Chapter 8: It's Not Safe	95
Chapter 9: I Need Help!	105

DEMOGRAPHIC-BASED BUTS

Chapter 10: I'm Too Old or Too Young	121
Chapter 11: You Can't Where I Come From	131
Chapter 12: I'm Not Qualified	141

PERSPECTIVE-BASED BUTS

Chapter 13: I Don't Feel Successful	155
Chapter 14: What Will Others Say or Think?	165
Chapter 15: What If I Fail?	175

YEAH, BUT... I'M NOT READY

1

Let's cut to the heart of this one right away. Are you ever ready? Think about your daily life and ask yourself that. Are you ready for that unexpected accident on the way to work? Are you even ready for your alarm to go off in the morning?

This is clearly an internal Yeah, But that you tell yourself and others. It also implies the answer: "No, I'm not," thereby already trapping you in a vicious circle of unreadiness.

Like most other Yeah, Buts, this one can't necessarily be removed and doesn't have a one-size-fits-all solution. The way of dealing with it lies in accepting that you may not be ready but asking yourself if that's reason enough for not taking the first step.

READINESS DEPENDS

To the extent that it exists, our readiness to do anything varies, depending on the thing to be done and the kind of person we are. Our personality type, our motivation levels, the financial costs involved, and even the riskiness of the situation can all play their part in determining how "ready" we can feel to achieve something. (See *Yeah, But... It's Not Safe*)

For example, when we pass our driving test, are we truly ready to drive unsupervised? The driving instructor thinks we're safe to do so, but we might not feel "ready." Some people will hop straight behind the wheel and head straight out on a road trip.

Others might beg their friends and family to come in the car with them just to drive around the block.

The same goes for anything else in life. Are you ever truly ready to do anything you've never done before? Is there ever a perfect time to become a manager or leader? Or be self-employed? Get married? Become a parent? Of course, sometimes the conditions are going to be more favorable than others, but in pretty much everything new you ever attempt, big or small, there's always a leap of faith, a step into the unknown.

Even though we might know this intellectually, it can still be hard to walk the talk. Not *feeling* ready is an excuse all by itself. You want to have everything ready, to get your ducks in a row first.

This Yeah, But can also manifest itself as a form of perfectionism. The conditions don't just have to be right; they have to be perfect. But if there's never a right time, how can there ever be a perfect time? The fact is, you might not have all your ducks in a row, no matter how much you try to control everything that's going on. There will always be tides and ripples that you can't do anything about.

WEIGHING THE COSTS

Not being or not feeling ready is a common Yeah, But across all areas of life. But rather than wading further into it by trying to gain more control over external factors or by trying to make everything just-so, is it possible to embrace heading in the opposite direction by taking the first step anyway?

One way we can reframe not feeling ready is by weighing the cost of diving in immediately against the cost of waiting and waiting because everything is not as you'd prefer it to be.

Of course, there are times when the former approach is not only preferable but also necessary. You wouldn't open a surgery center without doing any due diligence, figuring you can work it out as you go. You're dealing with people's lives and health (and you'd either get shut down right away or end up in jail).

But in non-life-or-death situations, would opportunities be missed if you took the latter route? Say you were starting a landscaping business. Should you wait until you've got the team and the equipment for major projects? Or would you be better off investing in a couple of mowers and starting with the basics, growing your skills, client list, and business from there?

Let's think about software developers. Imagine if they stayed in their offices and meeting rooms, locked in a never-ending cycle of development and refinement, forever waiting until their products were just right or until the "perfect" moment to launch them to the public. They'd never release a thing. And if they did, it would likely be dead in the water because another company would long have beaten them to the punch.

What they do instead is get their ideas out there in a usable form to a group of beta test users—people who don't work for the company. They can then act on feedback to fix bugs, improve usability, and iron out any other issues that real-world users have. This makes for a more engaged, organic approach to their product.

Adopting a beta mindset is often the healthiest way forward. By understanding that your project is an iterative, step-by-step process, not a long jump toward one ultimate goal, you can get started and often end up with a stronger, more rounded finished product than you would have done had you waited and waited for unattainable perfection.

"Better done and delivered than afraid and delayed."

*- **Wolfe**ism[2]*

CASE STUDY: *CHINESE DEMOCRACY* AND THE DANGERS OF CHASING PERFECTION

The creative arts are a great example of how doing this can end up working against you. In rock music, perhaps the most famous story is that of Axl Rose and Guns N' Roses. By the early 1990s, they'd become one of the hottest acts in the world, selling millions of records and touring the globe to sell-out crowds. But then they spent 15 years making one album.[3] Rose's notorious perfectionism meant that most of the original band members quit, and songs were recorded over and over again. There were endless legal wranglings, and costs spiraled.

By the time the finished product, *Chinese Democracy*, was released in 2008, it was reputedly one of the most expensive albums ever made, costing some $13 million.[4] However, the process had taken so long that, quite simply, the world had moved on. Sales were nowhere near those of previous Guns N' Roses albums, and the whole project was enveloped in an inevitable sense of anti-climax.

In other words, by trying to get everything perfect, Axl Rose lost momentum while simultaneously building expectations so high that they could never be matched.

CASE STUDY: QUIBI—TOO BIG TO FAIL? OR TOO BIG TO ADAPT?

Another, even more telling example is Quibi, a mobile-only streaming platform that was the brainchild of DreamWorks co-founder Jeffrey Katzenberg and one-time eBay CEO Meg Whitman. It was backed by major Hollywood players and raised $1.8 billion in funding.[5] Everything about its pedigree seemed perfect. It should have been too big to fail, but it went under in six months. And part of the reason was over-planning and over-committing.

When Quibi launched in April 2020, they thought they'd got all their bases covered: high-quality short-form programming for mobile users advertised using the best traditional methods.[6] What could go wrong?

But right around that time, the pandemic hit and lockdowns came in. Suddenly, people didn't want 10-minute bursts of programs on their phones. They wanted longer narratives on bigger screens. Katzenberg and Whitman can be forgiven for not foreseeing something so unprecedented, but other issues quickly became apparent with Quibi: there was no social-media share function, and users couldn't screenshot what they were watching. Great for exclusivity, but a major self-imposed disadvantage when it came to organic, word-of-mouth marketing.

In addition, paid subscribers who opted for the lower end of the two-tier subscription system were still expected to sit through advertisements when they could simply get free content with ads or ad-free paid content just as easily elsewhere. But Quibi had already sold $150 million of advertising space and invested too heavily in its all-original programming to be able to respond effectively.[7]

That October, despite increasingly desperate measures, including share options, free subscriptions, and the ability to play content on certain TVs, the platform shut down, with employees losing their jobs, programs left unfinished, and investors having lost well over $1 billion.[8]

TURN YOUR BUT AROUND

The key takeaway from Axl Rose's self-defeating quest for perfection and Quibi snatching defeat from the jaws of victory is that there can be a disconnect between what sounds perfect during the planning stage—what *should* work amazingly—and what is going to work in the never-predictable real world. One way to close that gap is to adopt a beta mindset and be willing to risk failure.

Okay, you might argue that Axl Rose couldn't change his album once it was out there, but would he have enjoyed more success (and been more creatively fulfilled) had he risked putting out an acceptable, less-than-perfect album, letting the fans enjoy it and decide, and then starting another album, rather than going over and over the same handful of songs and ending up overdoing them? We can only speculate that getting it done sooner might have allowed the band to avoid the secondary problems of members leaving and fans becoming disinterested.

Not only is waiting for the right, optimal, or perfect moment unrealistic, but it can also end up having the opposite effect of wrecking whatever it was you wanted to achieve.

So, how can we work past that? How can we get to a stage where we embrace the unknown and become willing to risk taking a misstep in order to reach our destination?

READY VS PREPARED

For me, the answer is a kind of compromise. If you feel like you haven't got as many elements aligned as you'd like, then ask yourself how many you'd need to feel ready to at least start moving forward. Doing that is, in itself, a step forward.

That's a very subtle shift right there: you accept that there are going to be challenges, and you've equipped yourself for most eventualities, but you're also maintaining a mindset that is prepared to adapt and adjust when needed. You're saying to yourself and your team, "This might not go perfectly the first time, but we've got enough to get going."

There's a small but crucial difference between being "ready" and being "prepared." Being ready can imply that you feel good to go. You're mentally in the right place to act, you believe you've got everything you need, and you can act right away.

Being prepared, on the other hand, implies that you're in the right place to act *and* respond to potential changes and challenges along the way. You can feel "ready" to climb a mountain, but if you haven't trained properly, checked the weather conditions, or even ensured that you've got all the proper equipment packed, then you're certainly not prepared. This applies equally to a project or a goal. You might have the mental readiness and eagerness to rush out and start making it happen, but you might not be properly prepared to see it through.

We touch on this subtle difference and the need for adaptability more in *Yeah, But… What's the Plan?*.

ACTION TODAY

Something I find people use with dismal results are New Year's Resolutions. "On January 1st, I'm fixin' to…" Why only then? Why are you waiting for that single, almost arbitrary point on the calendar to start taking positive action?

You can just as easily prepare yourself to change your habits on March 9th or August 23rd as you can on January 1st. The calendar has so little to do with it, and letting it dictate such changes delays what could be accomplished much sooner!

Procrastination can lead to what's known as "paralysis through analysis," where the constant waiting and planning can end up stopping you from doing anything. Ultimately, whatever your state of readiness, there comes a time when you have to say, "Okay, let's stop the debate now and *do* it!"

BUT BUSTERS

Progress trumps perfection. Every successful project starts with an imperfect first step. What's yours?

_____
_____
_____
_____
_____
_____

Does the prospect of success scare you? Perhaps you fear the responsibility, scrutiny, or potential change it could bring. Recognize that growth necessitates stepping outside your comfort zone.

_____
_____
_____
_____
_____
_____

Do you doubt your abilities, knowledge, or experience? Challenge those limiting beliefs! Remind yourself of past successes and focus on learning and evolving, not just knowing everything.

_____
_____
_____
_____
_____
_____

Remember, not every "not ready" is an excuse. Sometimes, genuine preparation is needed. However, by asking these candid questions and recognizing the insecurities that might be holding you back, you can empower yourself to move from "paralysis" to "progress."

_____
_____
_____
_____
_____
_____

What's the first step you plan to take now that you've read this chapter?

_____
_____
_____

Congratulations! You've started busting this Yeah, But!

YEAH, BUT... SOMEBODY ALREADY DID IT

2

You get a great idea and then find out that somebody already did it. Of course, they already did it. *Everything* has been done before in some way. "There's nothing new under the sun" is a quote from the Bible, which gives you an idea of how long people have been saying exactly the same thing!

Right away, then, we know that it's almost impossible to come up with something completely new, something that's never been done before. But what if we take a look at anything that has ever been made? Trace its origin and you'll find that it's an interpretation, an iteration, or a modification of something that already existed.

Someone writes a book on a topic—World War II, for example. There are thousands of books already out there on that topic, but more keep being published, and more importantly, people keep buying them. Why? It's a huge and fascinating topic, sure, but there's more to it than that. There are always new angles, different voices, and fresh discoveries that change how people think about certain aspects of the war. Beyond that, there's the timing of a book, how it's marketed, and who wrote it.

So we can see that it's shortsighted and self-limiting to say, "It's been done already." Equally, we can see the importance of having the ability and the confidence to say, "Sure, this is something that's been done before, but A) I know there's an audience for it, and B) I've done it a new way." From that new way comes a fresh perspective. And a fresh perspective is often as good as seeing something for the first time.

REINVENT THE WHEEL

"Somebody already did it" is a Yeah, But that you might be facing internally and externally. Why? Because you might discount your own ideas as soon as you have them, thinking, "Yeah, so-and-so did that." But did they? Did they do *exactly* what you want to do or dream of doing? Or are you adding your unique perspective, taking a very similar idea and moving it forward, even if only by a fraction?

You can also face the same criticism from others. You might present your idea, confident of its value, only for critics to say, "Don't reinvent the wheel." That's a phrase that's said so often that it's assumed to have inherent wisdom, but when you pause to think about it, it's misguided and means nothing. My response is always, "If we didn't reinvent the wheel, where would we be?" There's always room to advance. That's why patents have expiration dates—so that others can come along and try to improve them.

If you're still skeptical, let's think about tires. Ironically, they're the perfect example of why we *should* reinvent the wheel!

Have tires always looked like they do today? Of course not. The very first tires, which were invented thousands of years after the wheel, were metal bands strapped around wooden wheels to stop them from wearing away unevenly. Over the years, the bands began using other materials such as leather, rubber, and then synthesized rubber. Even the most modern tires are constantly being tweaked, improved, and advanced a little bit more every time. Developers are literally always reinventing the wheel. If they weren't, we'd still be rolling things around on stones. We need reinvention to evolve and survive.

WHY IS THIS A YEAH, BUT FOR YOU?

Generating fresh ideas in a world that appears full of them can seem like an unwinnable struggle. But guess what? Whatever industry or sector you're in, there's always scope. The door is never fully closed. That's why new songs are still constantly being written, even though millions already exist, and Western music only has 12 notes! Think about it: almost every piece of music you've ever heard, from Beethoven to Taylor Swift, is a reiteration of the same dozen notes, just played in slightly different combinations.

So, if you feel there's no space for you because everyone's already planted their flag on your soil, ask yourself if that's actually true. Somebody may well have already done something based on the same general ideas as you, but can you work *within* those parameters? Can you use what's there in a different way? Can you offer even a glimmer of a new perspective, especially to those telling you not to reinvent the wheel?

When you think about how an idea evolves, you realize how incremental the progress is—how it's often a case of one person saying, "What if we just added this one extra feature, if we just altered this, if we made this less expensive?" That's often all it takes to create differentiation and for the product or process to be seen in a new light.

Examples of this are all around us. The weight-loss industry is one of the biggest in the world. It's worth hundreds of billions of dollars every year, and it's growing all the time. And what is it? It's like music—variations on a theme: diets that are meat-heavy or meat-free, high-carb and low-carb, protein, Keto, fasting, blood type, the list goes on. Some might only slightly vary from what's gone before. Others might purport to present something completely new. However, all fall under the umbrella of "diets" and will have some link, however small, to other diets.

You might use popularity as an excuse to stay away from an idea—the market's too crowded; it's oversaturated—but you can also choose to look at it as being more palatable and worth getting into. Why do I say that? Because when you ride a marketing trend, you also have the opportunity to ride the wave of what people are already dealing with. Some trends last a long time, and others vanish overnight. Sometimes, like the home-baking craze during the pandemic, they're an almost random response to external factors. But whatever they are, you come away ultimately understanding that there's a way of capitalizing on it, of finding space to present something that people have been doing for years, maybe even centuries, in a new light.

In fact, we're surrounded by examples of this, like the craze of meal-kit delivery companies. Prepping food is nothing new—millions have been getting meals delivered for years—but now there's a more nutritious, diet-sensitive way of doing it. Again, the brilliance of the idea lies in its simplicity: taking something that people do every single day and turning it slightly so that it's seen afresh.

Here's an even simpler example: Marie Kondo has become world-famous as an "organizer." She has sold millions of books and built a business empire by writing about tidying up and keeping your house clean. It's inspired because it's the *antithesis* of new. It's presenting something that countless people do (or try to avoid) every day but in a slightly different light. That's something that *anyone* can do.

YOUR STORY IS UNIQUE

We can use this book as an example, too. It's far from the only book on overcoming obstacles, but I also know that no one else but me could write it because no one else has my exact combination of experiences, ideas, and insights. No one else could show you how to work through your Yeah, Buts in the same way that I'm doing here. Equally, although millions of other people will share the same Yeah, Buts as you, no one will have them in quite the same way. This means that whenever you read this book, what you take from it is unique as well. In that sense, we're constantly reinventing the wheel in almost every aspect of our lives.

No one made me write this book, and similarly, the onus is on you to tell your story to those around you. That could mean telling it to one person in a room or one million people online. Remember, there have been countless billions of humans before you, but none of them have the same story, the same experiences, the same thought patterns, or the same nuances that you do. You have something unique to offer, a detail to add to the big picture.

Your idea, your "end," may well be someone else's "means," and vice versa. Always stay open to possibilities and be prepared to adapt or change what's already there, however slightly.

Hopefully, you see now that it's time to move past the idea that you can't do something because somebody else has already done it. It's a given they already have. Those who say there's nothing new under the sun or tell you not to reinvent the wheel are stating the obvious, but there's more to life than the obvious. Sometimes a shift of just one degree can shed new light on the oldest and most established ideas. Stay alert to those kinds of shifts. Be aware of what's already out there. Keep an active eye on what's trending and what's on its way out.

> *"Let the gap become your map."*
>
> – **Wolfe**ism

CASE STUDY: TOUCHSCREEN COMPUTERS—A SOLUTION WITHOUT A PROBLEM... AT FIRST

Don't get hung up on the idea that change has to be drastic or discover uncharted territory. It doesn't. What you sometimes end up with in those cases is a solution looking for a problem.

Take the time Microsoft produced the Surface RT, a touchscreen tablet (with a detachable keyboard). It didn't catch on.[9] The same went for Apple's Newton (an early idea of what later became more widely known as a handheld Personal Digital Assistant (PDA), a physical device not to be confused with the current online understanding of PDAs).[10] Both suffered issues, and the buying public ultimately weren't invested enough in the idea to overlook these shortcomings so they didn't buy them. Both products failed. And even though the Surface RT ended up causing Microsoft to lose $900 million, it's the kind of story that we look at with hindsight and say, "They were way ahead of their time."[11] It's also why the most successful ideas often only change an existing solution very slightly.

Later, Apple returned with the iPad, which kickstarted the age of tablet computing. Nowadays, tablets are the norm. We see everyone using them, from little children to bank clerks. It's a thriving ecosystem, and it has irreversibly changed the way we use computers.

Of course, both Apple and Microsoft were only reinventing the wheel. Computers already existed. Apple and Microsoft just made them handheld. But the twist is that Apple succeeded after already trying and failing. The exact reasons for the initial failure and later success of handheld computers are complex, but their example illustrates that innovations don't always succeed on the first attempt. Most importantly, it's worth remembering that it happened because it's the kind of thing that can and will happen again.

So ask yourself what you've written off as being "impossible." Maybe it's time to take a fresh look and re-evaluate. Perhaps the timing wasn't right, the technique was off, the name wasn't right, or the marketing wasn't selling it properly. If it's something that you still think about, saying to yourself, "One day, I'd love to try that again," then maybe now the world has caught up with you. Your iPad-type idea may be waiting.

IT'S UP TO YOU

If you're reading this and thinking, "Yeah, that's all very well, *but* I've got no new ideas," then take positive action (see *Yeah, But… I Don't Know Where to Start*). Act contrary and see how shifting your usual, well-worn methods and routines can shake things up.

For example, being somewhere different from your normal environment might stimulate your thoughts and help you see things in a way you normally wouldn't. Do you usually work at home in a quiet office with the same four walls around you? Then, go out for a walk or work in your favorite coffee shop or co-working space for a morning and see what happens.

Alternatively, if you're always on the go and working in busy spaces where you're constantly bombarded with noise and people, then try getting somewhere quiet and allowing yourself to hear your thoughts more clearly.

Remember, everything I'm telling you here is for you to make your own choices. I'm not a math teacher telling you that if you add two and two, you'll get four. Take time to actively consider how you can make your journey uniquely yours. Mindmap creative ways to customize your experience. This act of reflection and ideation will help you push past doubts and objections by focusing on what you can proactively do to stand out. Putting these imaginative thoughts into action is key to rising above the Yeah, But mentality because others reading this book will be doing the same thing. Join them.

BUT BUSTERS

What if you present your idea differently from how others have presented it before?

_____
_____
_____
_____
_____
_____

Who is your audience, and what are their needs right now?

_____
_____
_____
_____
_____
_____

How can you make it more accessible, affordable, or usable?

_____
_____
_____
_____
_____
_____

What features or tweaks would make this relevant for today and even tomorrow?

_____
_____
_____
_____
_____
_____

What's the first step you plan to take now that you've read this chapter?

_____
_____
_____

Congratulations! You've started busting this Yeah, But!

YEAH, BUT… I DON'T HAVE TIME

3

This is one of my favorite Yeah, Buts. "I don't have time." Guess what? We all have 1,440 minutes in each day that we're alive. 1,440 minutes, each lasting 60 seconds. At that level, you, Bill Gates, and Jimmy Fallon are equal. You all get the same amount of time. It's up to you how to use it.

I call it the 1,440 Formula, where you create what you will do with your 1,440. It comes down to a simple choice: do you want to let time work against you, or do you want to make it work for you?

This particular Yeah, But is big on excuses. I can hear people angrily spluttering now. "Yeah, but you don't understand! I have kids! I have other responsibilities! Unexpected stuff keeps coming up!"

When we start turning this Yeah, But around, though, we're not denying any of that is true. On the contrary, we're taking ownership of it. We're saying, "Yeah, that's true, but…" and then we're looking at how you can make the time to get things done. You're not the only person who has other things going on. Just about every other successful leader and entrepreneur there's ever been has had a personal life, family life, and other commitments too. Do you need to live a solitary, monastic life to achieve success and see your plans through? Of course not. Is doing the grocery shopping or taking your kid to soccer practice a solid alibi for procrastination in other areas? Not really.

So, let's accept that you have many other demands in your life and start from there. Yeah, you probably don't have the time right now. But what are you going to do about it? How are you going to optimize those 1,440 minutes that you do have?

CASE STUDY: IGNAZ SEMMELWEIS AND MAKING TIME SAVES LIVES

19th-century Hungarian physician Ignaz Semmelweis is remembered by history for being an advocate of handwashing. At the time, doctors would rarely, if ever, wash their hands before delivering babies—even if they'd just performed an autopsy! Of course, women and newborns would then get sick and die of infections from what Semmelweis called "cadaverous particles" being passed on and postpartum infections developing. Yet prevailing wisdom insisted that infections and deaths were actually caused by "miasma"—bad air in the wards.

Semmelweis noticed that infection rates among newborns and their mothers were lower in wards run by midwives, who didn't perform autopsies, than those run by doctors. This discovery led him to advocate that doctors should wash their hands with a chlorinated lime solution before delivering babies.[12]

As logical as it seems to us today that you might want to wash your hands as you move between handling a corpse and delivering a baby, some doctors at the time opposed Semmelweis on the basis that doing so would waste valuable minutes. In other words, their response was, "Yeah, but I don't have time."

Thankfully, this particular Yeah, But was eventually overcome, albeit not completely in Semmelweis' lifetime, and some of the reasons why are discussed elsewhere (see *Yeah, But... I Need Help*). It's now taken for granted that people can and should make time to wash their hands. Few, if any of us, ever think about it. Even the most meticulous planners don't schedule time to wash their hands. They just do it.

This story gives us perspective. It also magnifies the potential benefits of making time and how something can become so embedded in our lives that we don't even have to think about setting time aside for it.

The inverse of this is when we routinely misuse many of our 1,440 minutes. When it comes to doing this, social media is one of the biggest distractions to ever emerge, if not the biggest. If you're honest with yourself, how many precious minutes have you wasted scrolling endlessly through YouTube, Facebook, Instagram, TikTok, or X? Oftentimes, you're probably not even taking in half of what you're seeing; you're just subconsciously looking for the next little dopamine spike and reducing your attention span in the process. When you *are* taking things in or posting pictures and statuses, you might subconsciously be seeking the positive reinforcement that comes from accumulating likes or taking the moral high ground.

Alternatively, you might fall into the comparison trap of seeing others' seemingly perfect lives and amazing achievements, damaging your self-esteem. You might even become addicted to the self-righteous outrage that comes with social media politics, deliberately seeking out content that angers or offends you in order to argue and point-score with strangers you disagree with.

A traffic light is only on red for, say, 30-60 seconds, but even in that gap, you see drivers reaching for their cellphones, checking their notifications, and needing the driver behind to beep their horn to get them moving again!

Special apps can track and tell you how long you're spending on your phone each day, and the results can sometimes be unnerving, especially when you realize you've spent an hour on Instagram and have nothing to show for it.

BEING THOROUGH ISN'T ALWAYS BEST

I have a client. Let's call him Rob. Part of his job involves submitting monthly reports to his company's board of directors. For a long time, Rob's reports were always very detailed, because he's a very detailed person, but he realized over time that the board didn't actually want that much detail and didn't even read half of what he gave them. He was pouring his time into producing brilliant, comprehensive reports that weren't even being looked at. He was going above and beyond, but it was doing no one any favors. Worse, it was wasting a fair amount of his 1,440 minutes.

Once he'd realized this, Rob began honing in on what the board actually needed to know, which was more detail about the issues and struggles that the organization was having. That way, they could get involved and help more. The other things that Rob had been going into great detail about, i.e. the company's successes, weren't the priority. With this in mind, he found a trusted graphic artist on his team, and she started creating infographics that more quickly portrayed the opportunities that the organization needed help with.

Rob had been spending time where he thought it was needed but hadn't recognized that not only could he better engage the board, but he also had the talent on his team to help him further optimize both his reports and his time.

BUMPT™

Want a way to make something important and memorable? Create an acronym. I have one called BUMPT™. It stands for *Best Use of My Prioritized Time*. If you want to push past this Yeah, But, then get real with yourself about what your BUMPT™ is. Who owns your time? Yep, you do. You get to decide what to do with it. Even if you work for someone else, you get to choose whether to go to that meeting, answer that call, or read that email. You even get to decide whether you show up or not. No one's physically dragging you out of bed and making you attend. Or at least I hope not!

I suggest you start thinking about how you spend each moment of your day. Work out where the leaks are, where time drips away. Do you squander minutes, or even hours, scrolling, reading the news, or half-watching a streaming video? If so, apply the 1,440 Formula and start reclaiming your precious minutes from things that are not adding anything positive to your day.

Just as importantly, are there things that seem to add value but are, in reality, just routines that you've gotten used to? When you attend meetings, what are you gaining from them? What's changing because you attended? What is being accomplished, and who owns the outcome? Or do you just show up because that's what everyone is expected to do?

We saw from the previous story that Rob was going above and beyond. That's often a desirable trait, except in his case, it was neither expected nor appreciated, and it actually left him unable to fulfill his more critical obligations to the company. Once he learned how to best use his time, however, he found gains in areas that had impact, and the other leaders noticed too.

> *"Should it be done now, next, near, or no?"*
>
> *- **Wolfe**ism*

The pandemic taught us that nothing is set in stone and that time can be gained. Suddenly, in 2020, many of us weren't commuting to work. We were working from home, working different hours, and working in different environments. Everything changed, and some of us gained a lot of time. Whether we used that time to our advantage or not is a different matter. Some people did. Others binged on series after series. So this reiterates that time isn't our enemy. Time just *is*. It's how we utilize it that matters—

just like money becomes problematic if we spend it unwisely. The irony is, however, that we often value money above time, even though time is limited and money is, theoretically at least, inexhaustible.

This is a vital point because time is an irreversibly diminishing asset. We could lose $1 million and earn it back again, but we never get a single second back once it's gone. None of the 1,440 minutes we waste today will carry over to tomorrow. Even the time spent coming up with excuses for why we don't have time is time that's lost and could have been better used.

We know how many minutes we have each day, but we don't know how many days we have. We know this, so why do we often act as if we have forever? There are two ways of approaching this fact. We can surrender to morbidity and say, "What's the point?" Or we can use the knowledge that we have right now and however many of today's 1,440 minutes are left and ask, "What would life be like if I treated time with the same reverence I treat money? What would be different?"

When we start thinking about time like we think about money, there's a potentially huge change. You spend money and get a tangible return. Well, what about if you invest your time the same way? What if you invest your time in doing something that moves you forward and adds value to your life? What would the potential yield be then?

That thinking is why this book exists. I've invested my time into writing because I believe it will reach and help more people than even my leadership coaching, workshops, and consulting do. It can impact more lives and reach people that I would never otherwise come into contact with. Is there more lucrative short-term work I could be doing? Maybe. But right now, this is my BUMPT™, one with a greater payback in so many ways.

At the end of this chapter, there'll still be the same old 1,440 minutes in a day. Hopefully, however, you'll be starting to take stock of your time and then take renewed ownership of it. Ask yourself what you're willing to stop doing so that you can make the time to do something else. If you're doing one thing and it's not your BUMPT™, you're not doing any of the other things you say you've not got time for.

BUT BUSTERS

What are the potential consequences of not "making time" for an activity or a change? Are there risks, drawbacks, or missed opportunities you might face?

_____
_____
_____
_____
_____
_____

What are the true costs of "not having time" compared to the true costs of "making time"? Are you giving up something more valuable by clinging to the belief that you don't have time?

_____
_____
_____
_____
_____
_____

Are you realistically assessing your priorities and time commitments? Could you identify areas where you can reclaim unused or unproductive time for this desired activity/change?

___

What small, achievable steps can you take to "make time," even if it feels limited? Even 10-15 minutes a day can be valuable, and consistency is key. What can you delegate, break down into tasks, or leverage technology to create efficiencies?

___

What's the first step you plan to take now that you've read this chapter?

___

Congratulations! You've started busting this Yeah, But!

CLIENT CASE STUDY:
DON BAHAM—SMALL STEPS IN THE RIGHT DIRECTION

Each chapter of this book looks at a singular Yeah, But and explores ways to move past it. Yeah, But… life is more complex than that, I hear you saying. It's not unusual to find yourself juggling multiple Yeah, Buts, especially when you're a leader or in any position of responsibility.

I want to illustrate this by talking to some of the clients I've worked with in my 25-plus years of consulting, particularly those I've worked with since moving my management consultancy firm to Tennessee back in 2010 and incorporating executive coaching into my work. All of them are highly successful leaders and professionals who've all had to work through multiple Yeah, Buts along the way. The first such person is Don Baham.

Don Baham is a Chief Information Security Officer (CISO) and Security Technologist. When he first came to me as a client, he was president of a tech company, but his chaotic existence left him feeling stuck. He felt like he just couldn't find enough time to manage his team, move the company forward, and spend enough time with his family. On top of that, he found he was comparing himself to his peers, feeling that he *should* be further ahead than he was. At the same time, he didn't feel ready to make any significant changes. But although he was stuck and full of Yeah, Buts, he was also doing okay by most people's standards—he was comfortably uncomfortable.

Don Baham's story highlights one complexity of Yeah, Buts. You may have many of them happening simultaneously on the inside, but on the surface, everything can appear to be going fine, maybe even great. When this happens, we can become victims of our own success because we worry that untangling our Yeah, Buts might rock the boat that we've fought so hard to get afloat in the first place.

Thankfully, Don didn't become such a victim. He realized that action was needed and that to get unstuck, he needed to make and then execute a plan for change that he could own. He hired me as his executive coach to empower him in that process. As a result, he left his president role and instead pursued his lifelong dream of becoming a C-level executive, dealing with how the company addressed their security and tech demands.

When Don first came to me for coaching, the three Yeah, Buts he was struggling with were, "I don't have time," "I'm not ready," and "I'm not sure what to do next." Obviously, he didn't frame them as Yeah, Buts at the time, but they were all evidently there and holding him back.

After helping Don define what he wanted to achieve and what was keeping him from getting there, one of the first things I taught him, as I teach so many of my clients, was BUMPT™ (see *Yeah, But... I Don't Have Time*). This helped him address his perceived lack of hours in the day to attend to everything in his life. "Everything's around prioritization, right?" he told me during our chat for my *The Yeah, But Podcast*. "I have a busy day job; I've got other extracurricular responsibilities; I've got a family." For Don, the important thing was to learn to prioritize everything in his busy schedule so that he wasn't constantly feeling like he was running out of time. Things that were low-priority or that he was doing even though he didn't need to could make way for things that either moved him toward his goals or, like his family, were meaningful and gave him joy.

Don is also a great example of how one Yeah, But can lead to another. He knew what he wanted to achieve, but he didn't feel ready or qualified to go out and achieve it because he didn't feel he had the time. The way he described his thought process during our interview showed how universal this kind of thought process is and how much even corporate presidents can constantly be asking questions and doubting themselves: "I feel like I do have a passion for this, but am I the right person to be speaking [about it]? Do I have anything of value to add to this conversation, to this topic? At times, I feel like I do, and other times, I don't. So I don't know. Is this the right time? Am I ready? Are other people going to find this valuable, or do I need to gain additional experience before I'm ready to dig into it?"

One of the ways that Don had worked through this Yeah, But was to "fake it 'til he made it". He'd used this technique in various areas of life that he wanted to move into but hadn't necessarily felt ready for, from his career to becoming a dad for the first time. However, just like we discuss in *Yeah, But… I'm Not Ready*, he'd already discerned the crucial difference between readiness and preparation. "I do think there's some preparation to make sure you are as prepared as possible to take on new challenges," he explains.

Once again, one Yeah, But merges into another: two questions Don frequently found himself asking were, "Yeah, but what's the plan?" and "Yeah, but what's next?" During the course of his career transition, Don discovered that he had a real passion for helping companies to not only improve their security and technology, but also their corporate culture. He and I have done LinkedIn Livecasts talking about issues related to team and corporate culture, and when I spoke to him, he was on the path toward incorporating this into his work, yet he still found himself tackling this Yeah, But.

"I've seen example after example of how *not* to do it," he explains of corporate culture. "How it can be something that is not prioritized and/or toxic. And the more examples I experience directly or that I hear about from peers, I just feel like there's something I can do to make that better for my team, for other teams, for other leaders. The frequency with which I'm encountering these cultural examples seems like it could be the right time to do something, but I don't know what the next right step is, and I feel a little bit stuck in that. I need some help, or just some time to think about, 'What is the next step?' or 'What is the long-term plan?' and then what are those next steps to take?"

These were Yeah, Buts that Don was still navigating, and if you're moving toward a goal, then that's natural—you always want to make sure that you know what the next step is and how it aligns within the overall plan. Remember, there are always going to be hurdles, unforeseen circumstances, and other events that necessitate a change of plan or a pivot.

One But Buster that Don was working on to help him navigate his Yeah, Buts was using positive self-talk. "I'm not great at staying in touch with my emotions—my wife will tell you that," he admitted. An aspect of this involved Don making time to reflect on where he'd come from, where he was at, and where he wanted to go next. By doing this as a written exercise on a regular schedule, he could see the progress he was making. This, in turn, motivated him to stay conscious and not slip back into old habits and routines. It reaffirmed his commitment to prioritizing his time and not doing things simply because they were easy and familiar.

"You're always going to have an excuse," Don says of working through one's Yeah, Buts. "And I'm lumping myself into that because I've come up with some doozies on what's going to prevent me from doing XYZ. It's really making a choice to make something change, to do something different. It's just getting started doing something, making forward action, taking a small step, getting 10 or 15 minutes of extra time away from your phone or away from something that's distracting you. That's a really small step, but I have found taking those very incremental, small steps has helped me make bigger changes."

Don's story ultimately gives us some core takeaways: even

little steps are still steps forward, and if you're not prepared to take them now, then when are you going to take them? Finally, addressing Yeah, Buts around time can open up worlds of opportunities because you can free yourself from wasting precious chunks of your 1,440 minutes so you can move forward with purpose.

YEAH, BUT… I DON'T KNOW WHERE TO START

4

Yeah, but you've already started! Accomplishing something doesn't start with the first physical act. It begins when you start *thinking* about starting. The thing, whatever it is, starts existing at that point, even if it's only as a notion.

I believe that we are all created with and for a purpose. The focus is therefore to take time to reflect on who we are, what we're meant to do, and importantly, *why* we're meant to do it—a goal should always contain enough reason or spiritual value for it to be worth pursuing. Is there an idea burning inside of you, something you see in the world that you believe needs to be solved, rectified, or changed? Or do you just have a longing to do it *because now is the time*? Either way, that's a start.

So, really, "Yeah, but I don't know where to start" is a paradox because you can only say it once you've started! It's like being stuck in traffic and saying, "I can't get going." Well, you're already going, just not as fast as you'd like.

This Yeah, But is one that we struggle with internally because the hardest part is getting started in your own mind. It's not that we don't know *what* to do, but more that we currently can't figure out *how* to take the first physical step. Or perhaps we're building reasons for why we can't start? And what a waste of energy *that* is!

You might paraphrase it as, "Yeah, but I don't have the experience/resources/network," but those can all quickly be reframed so that you're asking, "What experience do I need?" "Where can

I find the materials or resources?" or "Where can I meet the right people?"

An idea can seem overwhelming at the very beginning, as daunting as scaling Mount Everest. But I speculate that there are very, *very* few instances where you can't quickly get a handle on how to start by breaking it down into much smaller tasks.

EVEN THIS BOOK HAD ITS YEAH, BUTS

I feel you. I confess that it's taken me longer than it should have to even start writing this book, let alone finish it. There are many times in my life when I've seen something that could be done yet I created so many excuses. Of course, I knew *how* to write but didn't know where to start. I wasn't sure why people would listen to me talking about not starting. I had the idea and knew what I wanted to do, but I didn't feel like I had a unique angle.

But then I realized that it wasn't about me. It was about the topic. I realized that many of us feel and see things in very similar ways, and we want to feel that connection—we want to feel seen and understood. That gave me my starting point. It wasn't about me sounding unique. It was about me being honest and empathizing with people while also being able to offer ways past any roadblocks.

CASE STUDY: DR. JAMES NAISMITH AND A WHOLE NEW BALL GAME. SORT OF.

The case studies here are necessarily ones where people could easily have said, "Yeah, but I don't know where to start," but they didn't. Or if they did, they soon discovered ways around it.

The first example goes back to 1891 and Dr. James Naismith, who was working as an instructor at the International YMCA Training School in Springfield, Massachusetts. His supervisor wanted him to come up with a game that would keep students occupied indoors during the harsh winter. In other words, he wanted Dr. Naismith to invent a sport.

Now, of course, Dr. Naismith could've said, "Yeah, but where do I start?" That would be a logical response to such a huge task. But his genius was to start drawing on elements of existing outdoor games and repurpose them for indoor use. From soccer, he got the use of a round ball, and from lacrosse, the idea of passing and catching. He even drew on a childhood game he remembered called "Duck on a Rock," which involved throwing small stones at a bigger stone to knock it off the place it had been perched and therefore called for skillful and accurate throwing.

He didn't pull a whole new game out of thin air. Games already existed for him to draw upon, and he used them as stepping stones to get himself started. The end result was a sport you might have heard of: basketball.[13]

CASE STUDY: MAKING A MINIMUM VIABLE PRODUCT (MVP)

Let me give you another example by telling a story from my own life. Recently, I had an idea of something that could be changed and improved. I was thinking about how, often, clients and customers don't like giving video testimonials, or more specifically, they don't know how to start, particularly when it comes to documenting positive experiences. Generally, unless prompted, people seem more motivated to share negative experiences of companies. Who calls a customer service center to compliment good service, right? It's generally to discuss problems and complain.

I wanted to help turn this around by making it easier not only for people to leave video testimonials for businesses but also for businesses to receive them. I began working on the idea with our marketing partner.

The minimum viable product (MVP) we created was a guided exercise that allowed people who wouldn't normally record video testimonials to do so. We wanted people who wouldn't know where to start with such a task to be able to, and we wanted businesses to easily receive and share the videos. It could also work on a B2B level, with businesses able to give testimonials for other vendors that they have worked with.

The initial testers—a select few clients and business executives—were all honored to be part of the process. We learned far more from working through the process one step at a time and maybe making the occasional misstep than from saying, "Yeah, this is a great idea, but where do we start?" or even "Why should we bother?" and leaving it at that. We realized that the start had come with having the idea in the first place. The next step was to begin the iterative process of developing it to the point where we could test a client-facing version and get constructive feedback from potential users. We didn't get everything perfect the first time, but because we'd started, it became easier for us to create modifications while inside the process.

In a sense, every action was contained within the first step. That was the moment we moved from a road-blocked idea to a real-world process.

> **"Prioritization means choosing which problems or opportunities not to address today."**
>
> - **Wolfe**ism

THE POWER OF THE WRITTEN WORD

Ultimately, to bust this Yeah, But, you've got to take action, however small and insignificant it might seem at the time. I'm consistently advising my executive leadership clients that they've got to get their ideas out of their heads and onto paper (or a digital equivalent).

It sounds easy, but when you try it, you soon realize that it can be tough to translate the thoughts in your brain into words on a page—and I'm just talking about brain dumping here, scribbling down your thoughts and concepts without any regard for turning them into an actionable next step. Some people, myself included, might prefer to take advantage of voice-transcript technology and record themselves talking and then either listen or read back what was said (although, depending on the program you're using, this can sometimes be hilariously inaccurate). I do this because I can talk faster than I can type—I can keep up with my own thoughts, however disjointed they may seem at that moment.

Almost as a side note to this, we all know someone who says they can keep track of their schedule, their to-do list, and all their ideas in their head. The kind who taps their temple and says, "It's all up here." You might even do it yourself. But there has been enough research done now for us to know that our brains aren't the best place for storing or retrieving important information. They're easily influenced by our emotions and whatever else is happening around us—think of the times you've remembered an event differently from someone else who witnessed the exact same thing. There's also confirmation bias, the human tendency to favor information that reinforces our existing beliefs and can prevent us from seeing contradictory evidence. In short, our minds can easily distort even the most basic, impartial facts without our being aware. That's clearly not a recipe for success.

During the early stages of the pandemic, this was driven home when many people found themselves struggling to focus on what would usually be routine tasks, from attending a meeting to reading a book. Articles and research suggested that Cognitive Load Theory (CLT) was at play—we were so distracted by our routines being hijacked and the world being in such a heightened state of change that our working memory couldn't cope with everything it was being asked to adapt to. The result was brain fog and fatigue. CLT isn't restricted to the pandemic, either. Sometimes, when information is presented to us in certain ways—for example, too much all at once or with too little context—it can overwhelm us and leave us feeling like we don't know how to start assimilating it. We can potentially overload ourselves with too many unorganized strands of plans and ideas, too. That's why journals and electronic to-do lists are essential.

The point I want to stress here is that although thinking about something might be the start, externalizing those thoughts and beginning to organize them is a necessary next step. Yes, it's about starting, but it's also about continuing.

TOO MUCH CHOICE?

If you're feeling like you don't know where to start, it's perhaps worth asking yourself if you've got too many options in front of you. This is something I increasingly see people struggling with, regardless of their personal or professional status. Because of the extraordinary explosion in information and connectivity that we've seen this century, we now have more choices than ever when it comes to almost everything. Even something as simple as choosing a phone case or a bottle of water can leave us overwhelmed with different choices, different brands, different marketing slogans, and different price points. We can buy in-person or online, and we can choose from literally thousands of sources.

Sometimes, however, it's best to keep your choices refined. Less is more. So if you realize that you're telling yourself, "Yeah, but I don't know where to start," then consider if the reason why is that there are too many options on the table, and you're falling into paralysis by analysis. Can you narrow your options down and make life easier for yourself without sacrificing quality?

I said before that it's about starting and then continuing. That's a great segue into giving yourself a new perspective on this particular Yeah, But. It's not always just about doing something and achieving total success. It isn't all or nothing. Sometimes, it's about simply getting something done. It's about getting it out of your head and into reality. That in itself is an accomplishment.

Let's say that no one ever read this book. By starting it and seeing it through to completion, I've still completed it and learned from the process of conceptualizing, researching, writing, editing, publishing, and marketing it. That is something relatively few people ever achieve. It's said that everyone has a book inside of them, but I'd add that very few ever get around to making it a reality.

But this book has a far broader purpose than personal achievement. It addresses issues that other people go through and often avoid dealing with. I'm offering practical solutions to these issues and discussing them in a way that you and other readers will connect with. But I'm also learning about myself, the creative process, and the book-writing journey that I can take forward into future endeavors.

REMEMBER, YOU'VE ALREADY STARTED

Our new perspectives loop us back around to the top of this chapter. "I don't know where to start…" Yet you've already started because you've been thinking about it. Now, break it down. Brain dump in whichever way you feel is best so that your disparate, almost random thoughts and ideas are somewhere for you to read, listen to, and appraise. Then, work out the next step. I deliberately say next instead of first because, at this point, you're already on your second and third steps. You've started. You already have elements to look back on. You're on your way.

BUT BUSTERS

What small, tangible step can you take today to bring your idea one degree closer to reality?

_____
_____
_____
_____
_____
_____

How can you reframe your perceived lack of experience, materials, or network into opportunities for growth and learning?

_____
_____
_____
_____
_____
_____

What past experiences or existing resources can you draw upon as stepping stones to begin tackling your idea or project?

_____
_____
_____
_____
_____
_____

Are you struggling with decision paralysis due to an overwhelming number of options? How can you streamline your choices to make starting easier?

_____
_____
_____
_____
_____
_____

What can you learn from simply starting and taking action, even if the outcome isn't immediate or perfect?

_____
_____
_____
_____
_____
_____

YEAH, BUT...

What's the first step you plan to take now that you've read this chapter?

_____

_____

_____

Congratulations! You've started busting this Yeah, But!

YEAH, BUT… I DON'T KNOW WHAT TO DO NEXT

5

You don't know what to do next? Congratulations! You're further along than a lot of people get. Maybe you're even further along than you realize.

Think about it: if you've overcome not knowing where to start and a whole host of other Yeah, Buts, then reaching a point where you're thinking, "What do I do now?" is a significant milestone. You might even say it's a comparative luxury!

I get what it's like, though. It can feel like you're at a point where you've got yourself started, but then you have a wobble. You can compare this to so many things in life, from starting a business or speaking in public for the first time to getting a tattoo or a drastic haircut. You're halfway through the process, and then you suddenly realize that you're out of your comfort zone. Maybe you get a little stressed out and think, "What am I doing?!" That's normal human behavior, but the important thing is to remember that you're on your way.

SHOULD YOU KNOW IT ALL?

When you say that you don't know what to do next, are there perhaps implied additional clauses? "I don't know what to do next, but I should know, and I'll look foolish if I don't"? (See *Yeah, But… What Will Others Say or Think?*)

We often heap pressure on ourselves to instinctively know what to do next. After all, that's what happens in most of the success stories we read about: people follow their gut, do what they feel is right, and it all works out for them. So if we want to get past our Yeah, But and reach our goal, then it's natural to feel we *should* know what to do at every step. But how true is that?

It's vital to remember that everyone has a limit to their knowledge and experience. No one knows it all. There are times when we have to ask for help or a different perspective to find the next step, especially if we're trying to do something we've never done before. (See *Yeah, But... I Need Help*.)

It's equally important to remember that this incremental learning process never stops. As famous executive leadership coach Marshall Goldsmith says, "What got you here wouldn't get you there." And in many ways, that's the beauty of it: you're still on a journey, and you're still learning.

> **"It's not about the excuses you make but the actions you take."**
>
> — **Wolfe***ism*

CASE STUDY: THE THOMPSON PASS—WHEN INACTION ISN'T AN OPTION

Winter in Alaska is notoriously harsh, with 500-600 inches of snow falling in the Thompson Pass area of the Chugach Mountains—that's between 40 and 50 feet of snow every year.[14] That's obviously an incredible amount of snow, and it would be easy for local authorities to say, "Well, there's no way we can clear that."

But people need access to the area, and they need to get from one place to another. They can't be cut off and snowed in for months on end. So, over the years, specialist technology and protocols have been developed to ensure that, however bad the snow is, people are still able to get through.

Alaskan snowplows work using Differential GPS systems to aid Standard GPS. This means they use signals from ground stations to increase the accuracy of those from satellites. As a result, their onboard navigation systems are accurate to within inches of their position, meaning that the plow drivers can safely follow the virtual road on the screen in their cab and are able to drive during zero-visibility whiteouts.[15]

Of course, the plow drivers in Alaska receive rigorous specialist training, and the plowing system is highly organized and optimized, meaning that they can respond and adapt to even the heaviest of snowstorms.

This shows that there are times when action is needed. You've got to get from A to B, and throwing your hands up and saying, "I don't know what to do next" just isn't an option, even if you're snowblind.

But also, it illustrates that there will often, if not always, be obstacles in your way. Things are going to come up, and if you take note, then you can be prepared—you can always have *some* idea of what might be coming next. In Alaska, they know there's going to be a ton of snow and that solutions are required, so they plan accordingly, developing and acquiring the tools they need to combat roadblocks (literally, in their case).

CASE STUDY: NELY GALÁN—ADAPT AND THRIVE

Another example that shows the importance of taking positive action rather than letting events keep you at a standstill is that of Cuban entrepreneur and television producer Nely Galán.

Galán was born in Cuba but relocated to the United States with her family as a young child. A pivotal moment happened early on in her life when she was falsely accused of cheating on a high school test and the 'A' grade she'd achieved was taken from her. Although most people around her, including her parents, wanted her to accept the injustice and apologize, she responded by writing an essay about the scandal and sending it to the popular magazine *Seventeen,* based in New York. The magazine's editor was so impressed that she offered the young Galán a guest editor spot. The school also backed down on its accusation and gave Galán her 'A' back.

Galán went full-time with *Seventeen* after leaving school before moving into television work in her early twenties. She eventually launched her own production company, but unfortunately, it wasn't an immediate success. In fact, Galán didn't make a cent out of the company for four years. It was only thanks to the advice of a mentor that she eventually "remade" the company and began to enjoy success, particularly when she started bringing Latino stories to mainstream television audiences.

The success of Galán's company led to her being appointed the first-ever female President of Entertainment for the Telemundo network in the late 1990s. A few years later, Telemundo was acquired by NBC, and Galán moved on again, selling independent programs to major networks. Her continued success led to her becoming a TV star herself when she appeared on *Celebrity Apprentice.*

Galán's time in front of the camera led to her becoming a sought-after keynote speaker for Fortune 500 companies, which in turn started her on a path towards inspiring other women to become entrepreneurs and create their own destinies, work she continues to this day.[16]

What Nely Galán's story can teach us is that when it comes to knowing what to do next, we don't always need to be working from a set script or plan (see *Yeah, But... What's the Plan?*). Sometimes, events will unfold in such a way that they present potential next steps to us. We must take action to reach that point, and we always have the power to choose whether we take certain steps or not, but by remaining open and adaptable, we can always find a productive way forward.

AB2C: ALWAYS BREAK TO CLARITY

When we're talking about getting stuck during any part of a process, I always like to break to clarity. What does that mean? It means that when an obstacle appears too big to overcome, we start breaking it down into smaller and smaller sections until we find the next logical step, however small it might be. Even if it's one small step forward, it's still one step closer to where you want to be. It still reduces the distance between here and there.

Following on logically from this, another clever way of flipping it is to say, "What *can* I do next?" With the snowplow example again, there's a clear destination, an end goal: the road needs to be cleared. In your own life, once you've defined a similar clear goal, see if you can say to yourself, "What things can I put around me that will allow me to get moving, to clear the road ahead?"

When you're going through this, don't just think about physical resources. What other assets do you have around you that you might be underutilizing? Without overwhelming yourself to the point of paralysis through analysis, do you have any data available? Are there any examples of people who've achieved similar things before?

Sometimes, we need data to tell us things that we can't see for ourselves. The snowplow drivers in whiteouts are an example, and so too are airplane pilots. When a pilot is flying a plane, they might not be able to see everything around them. When trained and certified, however, pilots can fly "instruments only," meaning they can guide their aircraft perfectly safely using only onboard readings. They don't need to look out of the cockpit window for visual clues as to where they are and how high they are.

We can't know everything, and we can't see all the variables. But as long as we know where we want to arrive, we can usually find sources to help us plot the way, even if it's not always clear, which it likely won't be. The route to the top of a mountain is seldom straightforward, but that doesn't stop mountaineers from climbing. They know that their success depends on them persevering and finding a way to the top. And that's the kind of mindset we need to develop if we want to navigate the Yeah, Buts in our path.

It's important to understand both perspectives if you're ever stuck on what to do next and want to make an honest assessment. And that word honest is crucial here because, without it, you're liable to either under or overestimate potential risks. (See *Yeah, But… It's Not Safe*)

We can do this by formalizing the idea of breaking to clarity into a simple rule: Always Break to Clarity (AB2C).

Start by writing down your primary end goal, however far away it seems right now. Then, start breaking it down into smaller, more manageable steps. If the steps you're looking at take weeks or months to complete, then they're still too high-level, so keep breaking them down until you're measuring steps in terms of days or even hours. They're far more tangible and manageable than longer stretches of time. Keep assessing what you need to complete each step (acquiring what you need for a certain step can become a step in itself) and work until each step is approximately the same size. If you've got one step that seems much larger than those around it, then it can likely be further broken down. Eventually, you'll arrive at a point where you've got honest, realistic, logical steps laid out in front of you.

Once you're done, you should have gained clarity on what your end goal is and how to reach it, one step at a time. Not only that, but you'll also have taken the next step, *and* you've worked out what the step after that should be! A further potential bonus is that you might realize you're further through the process in question than you thought you'd be.

KEEP GOING

Often, forward motion is better than no motion, so long as it's relevant. Even when you feel like you've got a lack of clarity and things seem to be moving at a snail's pace, it's still better than getting completely stuck.

Remember too that if you get stuck in a whiteout—you can't see any way forward—and you don't know what to do next, then there is another step there. It's implicit in what you say: I don't know what to do *next*. That means that there is at least one step that can be taken. How can you change your perspective so that you start seeing it as a matter of adapting and adjusting?

Not knowing what to do next is different from being in a dead end. You can take stock of your process and the people you have around you and see if you have everything and everyone you need to help take you forward. Can you even use the 10-10-10 strategy[17] described in *Yeah, But... It's Not Safe* and work out what things will look like once you've moved forward? Doing this alongside the AB2C strategy described above may help you to work out what to do next.

BUT BUSTERS

What does getting unstuck look like? As a metaphor, think about how much snow before you must go.

Know your ABCs: Always Break to Clarity (AB2C).

_____

When was the last time you paused and measured how far you've come to reach where you are now? How many little steps have you taken?

_____

What does getting unstuck look like to you?

_____

What's the first step you plan to take now that you've read this chapter?

_____
_____
_____

Congratulations! You've started busting this Yeah, But!

YEAH, BUT… WHAT'S THE PLAN?

6

Okay, you've set your goal and you know what you want to do. How are you going to get there? What are the exact steps from where I am to where I want to be? What's the plan?

If only life were that simple—the plan was ready and written, and right from the start, you just had to follow the steps and everything would simply fall into place. However, we all know, or we should all know, that's rarely, if ever, the case. Plans are always changing and evolving, and to have any chance of success, we have to change and evolve with them.

Think about it like a road trip. You know your destination, you've packed everything you'll need, and you've got a full tank of gas, but then, within 100 miles, a section of the highway is unexpectedly closed. Do you stop and turn back, plow through the safety barriers, or take an alternate route? I'd say you're most likely to do the latter. It can be seriously frustrating that you've had a setback and your original plan needs to be altered—it can even make you feel like giving up and turning back, but your only chance of getting to where you want to go is to accept the variables that life throws at you and adapt to them.

I get that this can be a tough one to balance. If you rush into something without having any kind of plan whatsoever, then you're going to hit roadblock after roadblock. Plan too meticulously and refuse to alter course, however, and you'll also hit roadblock after roadblock. So, how do we define a healthy medium?

Former US President and five-star Army General Dwight D. Eisenhower famously said, "Plans are worthless, but planning is everything."[18] And that's worth taking a moment to unpack. In its original context, Eisenhower was talking about war and how even the most seemingly perfect plans can quickly go wrong as soon as armies start trying to implement them in real life. The most important thing, therefore, is planning–the ability to respond quickly and nimbly to events and to change course if necessary.

We're not discussing warfare here, but Eisenhower's main point resonates with my experience of working with executives. I've found many times that they need to be highly agile and responsive. They need to remain focused on the goal but hold it lightly to the point that they can work with the ebb and flow, moving and adjusting accordingly.

CASE STUDY: MICROSOFT COURIER–A TABLET TOO HARD TO SWALLOW

The use of minimum viable products (MVPs) illustrates this well. Once a company or a developer gets an MVP out into the real world for people to test, it allows them to get feedback, which allows for further adjustments, improvements, and iterations. When a company waits and waits, shrouds everything in secrecy, and believes that they alone have the perfect plan to create the perfect product to unleash on the world at the perfect time, things invariably go wrong.

Let's consider Microsoft Courier, an early example of computer tablet technology that never got further than the prototype stage and whose very existence is still cloaked in mystery to this day. The concept behind the Courier was the creation of a two-screen tablet that could be folded like a book and enabled users to keep handwritten notes alongside saved images and articles from the internet.

Courier was such a closely guarded project that no one knows exactly when development began, although it's estimated to be around 2001. Only a few trusted engineers were allowed to know about it, and no MVPs were released for feedback. In fact, Microsoft only officially acknowledged its existence in April 2010 in a statement that confirmed it was canceling the project.[19]

Just over three weeks before that fateful announcement, Apple had launched its first-generation iPad, which revolutionized the tablet market.[20] Although Apple was just as secretive about its product development, the release of the first iPads allowed the opportunity to get feedback ahead of the second iteration of the iPad, released just 11 months later. Microsoft had fallen way behind and wouldn't bring anything to the tablet market until the fall of 2012, by which time Apple had asserted its dominance.[21]

It was later revealed that Microsoft had handicapped themselves by over-planning the product and being too ambitious.[22] Rather than taking the technology they already had and tweaking it, the design team had elected to build a product using brand-new tech. They even wanted to do away with the familiar Windows operating system that consumers would have been familiar with, building a brand-new custom one instead. This radical approach led to clashes with senior executives, ultimately resulting in the product being shelved–right at the moment when the tablet market burst into life.

So, what can we take from this? Well, it doesn't matter if you're one person or a global tech icon, if your plan is too complex or too inflexible, or if you wait too long to get your MVP out there, someone else is going to beat you to the punch. After that, unless you can truly make your marketing stand out, then you're going to have a significant struggle.

> *"Preparation and perspective help lead to positive outcomes."*
>
> - ***Wolfe**ism*

THERE IS NO PERFECT PLAN

Investment experts like to say that it's about getting started and investing over time—there is no perfect time to start investing, and there is no perfect plan. It's all about *planning*, about moving in stages or increments. You can break your large end-goal down into a series of smaller goals, each of which acts as a building block toward your final destination. This isn't just about making things more manageable; as you achieve each of your smaller goals, you gain a fresh perspective. When you take things one step at a time in this way, you're also maintaining a degree of agility and constantly taking one step beyond any limiting ideas you may have had about what you thought was possible.

I can offer a personal example of this. When it comes to writing this very book, I've gained a far deeper understanding of what it is I want to get across by actually sitting down and writing it than I did when I was pontificating about what I *planned* to write. In fact, what was originally meant to take me just a few months to put together has ended up taking almost a decade. It's not that I didn't have a plan; I had one of those, alright. The problem was that, like Microsoft with their Courier device, I'd over-planned and over-thought the whole thing. In fact, I ended up with so many Yeah, Buts that I almost didn't write it!

I've also learned about the consequences of not seeing a plan through to completion. Early on in the process, I told people around me about why I was writing this book, the impact it would have on my target audience, and what would happen if I didn't see it through. Recently, some of those people started asking if I was working on my second book yet. Well, no, I was still struggling through my first.

It was then that I felt the weight of not having fully executed my plan. I also realized that this project had become more than a book. It had given me a sense of responsibility. I needed to take everything that I had learned and help people get past their Yeah, Buts. Remember, version one is better than version none.

A plan is like anything in life—you can only fully understand and respond to it when you're committing and engaging with it rather than just thinking and reading about it. There is no substitute for lived experience.

WHEN 'PIVOTING' SOUNDS LIKE A DIRTY WORD

One aspect of being flexible and responsive with your planning is the dreaded pivot. In the business world, it's a concept that gets thrown around pretty easily. Something goes wrong with your plan? Pivot. Your goal becomes unachievable? Just pivot to another one. Simple.

The problem is that the mere suggestion of pivoting in this sense can feel like a personal insult, a casual dismissal of your long-cherished goals and your burning desire to achieve them. This is your ship, sailing a course you've painstakingly plotted, and heck yes, you're going to weather whatever storms come your way.

If this sounds familiar, then trust me, you're not alone. We've all been there. You put everything you have into an idea, convinced that this is it—this is the golden ticket. But then reality suddenly throws a wrench in the works. Maybe you don't get the funding you need, or the market shifts, or a rival beats you to it. Suddenly, the path that seemed almost divinely clear and illuminated becomes blocked by a huge landslide.

This can be tricky territory to navigate, as it can lead to a battle between head and heart. Should you dejectedly accept defeat and pivot to another goal, or plow on regardless, grimly determined to reach your original destination at all costs?

Before you choose the latter path and almost certainly steer your ship onto the rocks, pause and consider this: pivoting away from your original destination isn't about abandoning your dream; it's about adjusting the sails to catch a different wind. It's about having the strength and the courage to realize that, sometimes, even the best-laid plans need to be altered.

We spoke earlier about the difference between plans and planning, and the important thing to remember is that plans are, in a sense, attempts to predict the future—they are frozen in time, based on what quickly becomes outdated information. Refusing to acknowledge the ever-changing business landscape or marketplace you want to apply your plan to is as counterproductive as stubbornly refusing to adjust your ship's sail when the wind changes. Awareness of your surroundings as they actually are, not as you want them to be, is essential.

It's also worth remembering that pivoting does not necessarily entail changing everything. Sometimes, even a minor tweak in your approach—a shift in your target audience or a slightly different marketing strategy—can mean the difference between floundering and flourishing.

The ability to discern constructive feedback and take it on board is also crucial (we look at the difference between constructive and destructive feedback in *Yeah, But… What Will Others Say or Think?*). As much as an idea or project might be your baby, and as passionate as you might be about completing it in a certain way, you'll inevitably have your blind spots. If there are people around who can see something that you can't, then it's vital to listen to them.

A great example of this is the late Steve Jobs' initial refusal to allow third-party apps on the first iPhone, released in 2007. Today, the notion that you might not be able to install WhatsApp, Paypal, X, or pretty much any major app on your phone is unthinkable, but back then, Jobs was worried that non-Apple products would cause issues with bugs and potentially harm his company's integrity.

Thankfully, he was encouraged by one of his senior vice presidents and a member of Apple's board to change his mind. He soon realized the wisdom of doing so, and so when the second iteration of the iPhone, the 3G, was released in 2008, its users were able to download third-party apps. Everybody benefited, and Apple retained control of what was available via their app approval policy.[23]

In short, pivoting is not a dirty word, and it isn't a synonym for failure. It's a strategy that allows you to keep moving forward when your initial plan doesn't match up with how events transpire.

STRATEGY AND EXECUTION

It doesn't matter if we're talking about books, digital tablets, or something completely different; if you've got a goal you want to reach, then as well as having a plan, you will benefit from focusing on two things: strategy and execution. Everything else, and I mean *everything*, pales into insignificance against these two things. You have to cycle between the two, constantly re-evaluating your strategy and honing your execution. Measure, refine, and repeat.

And above all else, remember that the path is seldom straight. It meanders. There are blind turns and hidden pitfalls, but if you're on that path, you're still growing, learning, and moving in a positive direction, even if it's by learning what *not* to do. As we discuss in *Yeah, But… What If I Fail?*, you fail forward. Each step, be it hard or easy, big or small, is both a reason to celebrate and be proud of yourself and a chance for you to evaluate and refine your strategy.

BUT BUSTERS:

Think about your goal. What incremental move could you make to move yourself one step closer to achieving it?

___

___

___

___

___

Is there another area of your life where you do not have a rigid plan but have made progress regardless?

___

___

___

___

___

How could you celebrate having moved one step closer to your goal?

___

___

___

___

___

If you decide to pivot, what upside can you find to show it as progress and a natural function of forward motion?

_____
_____
_____
_____
_____
_____

What's the first step you plan to take now that you've read this chapter?

_____
_____
_____

Congratulations! You've started busting this Yeah, But!

CLIENT CASE STUDY:
KEVIN DOSTALER AND THE VALUE OF KNOWING WHEN TO BE LED

For many years, Kevin Dostaler worked as a Certified Public Accountant (CPA). It was in his nature to be suspicious of change and to dislike vagueness. Everything in his life had to add up. I know Kevin well, so when he came to me a few years ago and told me he was thinking about quitting his steady accounting job to become a Chief Financial Officer (CFO) for one of his employer's clients—a role he'd never done before—I knew that it was a life-changing move for him. I also understood that there would likely be Yeah, Buts to work through.

However, because of how well I knew Kevin, I was reassured that he wouldn't be considering such a leap if he wasn't driven by a higher purpose. Like myself, he is a committed Christian and has always been led by his faith. This means that, despite his fear of change, he does sometimes take action that makes him feel uncomfortable. In this case, however, it turned out even better than he could have planned.

I know this because once Kevin had made the move, his new boss hired me to help coach him as he transitioned from CPA to CFO. Among other things, I was able to guide Kevin through any Yeah, Buts as they arose. I spoke to him recently about those days for my *The Yeah, But Podcast*.[24] I asked him what he remembered about that period and what he learned about overcoming his Yeah, Buts.

Kevin had been working as a CPA for several years. As we've seen in all the other client case studies, this alone is a notable achievement. But then he started to have thoughts of moving on. These were somewhat uncharacteristic for him, as he freely admits he doesn't like change.

Naturally, then, Kevin answered these thoughts with Yeah, Buts. "One of my Yeah, Buts was, 'I don't want to leave these guys; I've got all these clients I serve,'" he admits. "Maybe I was thinking a little bit too highly of myself that somebody else wouldn't be able to do that." But then events took an unexpected turn: "I had a major client that I serviced, but they left for reasons unrelated to me, so a big part of my service provision went away. I was like, 'God took away a big portion. He didn't nudge me out the door with a layoff, but he provided me an opportunity where I could leave and it might be softer on the employer that I'm exiting.'"

For Kevin, this was a sure sign that he should listen to the Lord. "I've got notes that I've written to myself because you kept telling me to write things down about this, and they're dated about six weeks before I took the CFO position," he explains. "And they're basically a bunch of Yeah, Buts! The first thing I wrote down was, 'If you are not praying, it means you are relying on yourself more than you're relying on God.' That was one of the things that contributed to me being on that path to change the guy who doesn't like any change. My thinking was, 'I've got this job. I could do this forever and be comfortable and be fine, but maybe there's something more.' I wasn't unhappy at my job, but I said, 'I need to be listening to God more.' And if I did this, if I made this change, I would not know what I'm doing. So, I would need to have Him tell me what to do. And I would need to listen to Him more. So that was a big step."

Kevin had never been a CFO before, and he was upfront with his potential new employer that he wasn't talking to anybody else (not a standard salary negotiating tactic!), but he was praying to God and seeking the opinions of others he respected. Through this process and later reflection, he realized that he was dealing with the flipside of most of the Yeah, Buts we deal with in this book: I *don't* want to do this, but...

"A lot of us say we want to do what God wants us to do, but do we really?" he asked me. "It's hard. In this case, He was telling me all these things [and to] get out of my comfort zone, which I hate to do. And I was like, 'I don't want to do this, but God wants me to.'"

Kevin felt guided by a higher power, but there were still risks and Yeah, Buts to conquer. He knew enough about himself to know that he was in a comfortable position. He could have stayed a CPA for the rest of his career, earning good money and secure in the knowledge that he had a job for life, something increasingly hard to come by as the 21st century progresses. His wife, while supportive, was uneasy with the proposed change because of the potential threat to their financial stability.

But whenever Kevin worried that he might fail or that he wasn't qualified to make this kind of leap, he kept faith. He remembered that he wanted to serve others, and this was how God wanted him to do it. "You have to listen to God, which is hard to do," he says emphatically. "Then you have to obey, which is hard to do. There are consequences. There are consequences if you do listen, there are consequences if you don't listen. Trust in God and He will handle the consequences."

Kevin ultimately took the leap and became a CFO. Immediately, he was up against new Yeah, Buts, and it's at this point that the company's CEO hired me to begin working with him in an executive coaching capacity. "My biggest [Yeah, But] was, 'Yeah, but I don't know what I'm doing,'" he recalls. "You helped me at that point because you told me to write out my story."

Kevin's job title was CFO, but he soon discovered that his role also encompassed tasks more typical of a CEO. Looking back now, he says, "What was great about it was, all I had to do was hang out with people and talk to them, listen, and help. A lot of it wasn't even financial; it was just helping them do their job. What was strange about it was, because of my position, people tended to listen to me more than in prior jobs. So it was an opportunity to speak to people boldly, and I did."

The move turned out better than Kevin could ever have anticipated, professionally, personally, and financially. Such is the strength of his faith that his sense of peace in following the Lord's guidance helped him to overpower his Yeah, Buts. "I just felt like I belonged," is how he describes it.

Kevin no longer works at the company but for very good reasons. In December 2020, just a little over five years after he took the leap, they were bought out by a company worth $700 million. Again, they asked me to help them prepare and illuminate opportunities for improvement that they were missing, both as individuals and as a team.

Although he's a qualified accountant, it's not always about financial incentives for Kevin: "If money is not your driver, the risk of leaving is like, 'I got to where I'm at. Why move?' But I know for myself that it's because there are other people you're supposed to help. If you stay here, you're not going to do what you could do if you move."

"Your book is all about Yeah, Buts," he told me. "And there are so many people where it just sits in the back of their minds, and they don't even think about it. They don't think about what God wants them to do. And they should. It's almost like a pail of crabs—when somebody's trying to crawl out, the others pull them back in. A lot of people aren't even climbing that wall or thinking about it, but a lot of people are, which is why this book's so good about overcoming bad habits."

As a Christian myself, I know my purpose and who I am led by. I appreciate that each of us is led by something, religious or otherwise. Whatever it is for you, clearly define it, lean into it, and act like your life depends on it. Because it kind of does. What are you going to do with what you have, and who benefits if you share your gifts even more widely?

YEAH, BUT… I'M NOT SURE I CAN DO IT

7

You know the old saying, "Whether you think you can or you think you can't, you're right." You probably know it so well that you haven't stopped to think about it for a while. When you do, realize that it's so true. When you say to yourself, "I'm not sure I can do it," you unknowingly edge yourself closer to not being able to do it.

What if we can reframe it? Think back to a time when someone told you, "I'm not sure you can do it. I don't think you're up to it. I don't think you've got what it takes." What was your instinctive reaction? Was it to shrink back and think, "They're right. I can't do it? or was it to come out fighting and think, Oh yeah? I'll show you?"

Now, apply that thinking to your inner critic. The beauty of taking on this Yeah, But is that you're working to prove something to yourself first as much as to anyone else. Can you get it off the ground? Can you see it through? Is it even possible? Unless you try and find out, you're pretty much just guessing and relying on your beliefs about whether you think you can or can't do it. If you want facts and evidence, there's one way to get them: to decide and then act. For all you know, the scope of your abilities could be way beyond what you currently believe yourself capable of.

There is, obviously, a line between self-belief and self-delusion, and we can all think of people we've worked with who've crossed that line. There is always a healthy amount of doubt, and it's okay not to be 100% sure you can do something, but it's a numbers game: the more confident you are, the faster you'll be able to act and get things accomplished. The more doubt that creeps in, the more it slows you down to the point of getting stuck.

It doesn't have to be a tightrope, though. The path of feeling sure while acknowledging doubts is broad enough to move along with the confidence that you don't fall off either side.

ARE YOU BEING REALISTIC? THE ROOTS OF IMPOSTER SYNDROME

A big reason for wanting to get this particular Yeah, But reframed and overcome is the dreaded Imposter Syndrome, which we discuss in more detail in *Yeah, But... I'm Not Qualified*. It's relevant here too, however, because Imposter Syndrome re-enforces and amplifies the voice saying, "Yeah, but I'm not sure," way above any reasonable level, and it can get you absolutely stuck. If left uncontained and unchallenged, it can even herald the beginning of a downward spiral for leaders.

However, before we even get to Imposter Syndrome, there are six personality traits that can lay the grounds for it to manifest. All are based on a perceived need to meet unrealistic standards, and they're worth considering on their own.

- The **perfectionist** sets themselves impossibly high standards.

- The **superhero** feels they must excel in every area of their life, have everything under control, and meet every expectation, real or perceived.

- The **natural genius** believes that they must do everything quickly, intuitively, and flawlessly. Any effort beyond that equals failure.

- The **expert** wants to know everything before starting a new challenge and is terrified of being seen as unknowledgeable.

- The **soloist** is convinced that they must achieve everything alone and that asking for help is a mortal sign of weakness.

- The **self-sabotager** is afraid of what will happen if they succeed. They don't feel capable of handling the higher expectations associated with success and subconsciously sabotage their chances of success.

When we recognize these aspects showing up in our work or our lives, then it's time to challenge them by reframing how we perceive ourselves. We can do this by being realistic about our expectations and our abilities, perhaps breaking our long-term goals down into smaller, more manageable goals. We discuss this in more depth in *Yeah, But… What's the Plan?*.

"LET'S SEE…"

There are often multiple ways of overcoming a Yeah, But—especially one that exists exclusively in your mind. If reframing your uncertainty as a chance to prove something to yourself doesn't resonate, then another way past it is to regard your uncertainty in a different, more positive light. "I'm not sure I can do it" can equally be phrased as, "Let's see if I *can* do it." Same scenario, maybe even the same level of uncertainty, but with a crucial pivot from a 50% chance of failure to a 50% chance of success, allowing you to start moving forward, however incrementally.

THERE'S NO SUCH THING AS STANDING STILL

We're generally talking about beginnings here. We can't achieve anything unless we get started. The world is spinning, so if we're not moving forward, we're going backward. You could say it's a law of nature that even when we fail, we have the opportunity to view it as failing forward. Even if we feel like we're back at square one, we can reflect on our experiences, learn from our mistakes, and use that knowledge to improve our future efforts.

Time never stops. It never even pauses. There's always something going on. Opportunities are always being presented, and momentum is always being created. It's on you to get involved and to make the most of the chances that are there and of the movement that is constantly happening. It might mean adapting and adjusting your plans as you roll, but with a mindset that says, "I'm going to prove something to myself," or, "Let's see where this goes," you're more likely to make a start, which instantly gives you a higher chance of success than not starting at all. (See *Yeah, But… I Don't Have Time*.)

POSSIBLE, PLAUSIBLE, OR PROBABLE?

When we adopt a "Let's see" mindset, we embrace the fact that we're dealing with unknowns, which I like to split into three categories: what is possible, what is plausible, and what is probable. They're similar adjectives, but they mean different things:

- **Possible** means something could happen, even if it's unlikely.

- **Plausible** means that something seems reasonable based on current knowledge.

- **Probable** means something is likely to happen based on evidence or past experience.

All describe different levels of likelihood. But crucially, even the least likely—when something is only possible—is not inconceivable. The potential for what you want to achieve does exist. It *can* happen, and with the right actions, it can become ever more plausible, moving up through increasingly probable until it happens. But even when a goal is less than possible, it's not an automatic game-over.

"YEAH, BUT IT'S IMPOSSIBLE."

Sometimes, self-doubt can feel like an obstacle course. You overcome your first obstacle only to find another, even bigger one blocking your path. You might successfully reframe your "I'm not sure" but suddenly hear someone say, "Yeah, but what you want to achieve is impossible." It could be a peer, a colleague, or worst of all, your inner voice.

This is a Yeah, But that's worth looking at closely because, on the face of it, it seems like a checkmate, a total *gotcha!* And if you let it remain so, then yes, it will be devastatingly strong. But when you break it down and look at real-world examples, you begin to see that it can also be an illusion.

Impossible is a word best approached one step at a time. Even if something is currently completely impossible, there are still steps that you can take and questions you can ask:

- If the end goal is currently impossible, what's the closest thing to it that *is* possible?
- What am I trying to achieve? To invent something brand new or improve on an existing idea?
- Would simply having a dialog about potential innovations create a positive impact?

You can see from these questions that there are actions and decisions you can make, even thoughts you can generate, to make even the impossible seem a little more plausible.

> *"What's possible when you 'stop missing the listening?'"*
>
> *- Wolfeism*

THE AMAZON EFFECT

There are many real-world examples of this process out there, some of which we can only awe at as spectators and some of which have made a tremendous impact on our day-to-day lives. A great example of the latter is online shopping. It's the norm now, but who would have thought in the early 2000s that people would not only buy almost anything online but also get it delivered to their door within 24 hours for "free?"

The majority of us would have called it impossible—the logistics, the infrastructure, the sheer cost. But over just a few years, it happened. First, it was free shipping if you spent over a certain amount, which quickly became standard practice. But in 2007, Amazon went one step further and unveiled unlimited 24-hour free shipping for those paying for an Amazon Prime subscription—of which there are now more than 200 million worldwide.[25] By centralizing their supply chain and gradually investing in enormous "fulfillment center" warehouses, Amazon changed the face of shopping. To consumers, it likely happened so quickly that it felt like a revolution, but it was an incremental process, with each step making the seemingly impossible plausible, then possible, then probable, and then a reality.

Today, same-day or next-day delivery has quickly become the industry standard alongside free shipping. Something that would have seemed like science fiction to us in 2001 became an indispensable part of everyday life within 20 years.

CASE STUDY: THE FIRST LADY OF STEAK AND THE POWER OF SELF-BELIEF

Amazon achieved the seemingly impossible on a structural level, but if we want to look at someone who didn't let this Yeah, But stop them from overcoming huge odds on a personal level, then we need look no further than Louisiana entrepreneur Ruth Fertel.

Fertel is best known as the woman behind Ruth's Chris Steak House, a worldwide chain with over 150 outlets bought by Darden Restaurants in 2023 for over $700 million.[26] And it all began because Fertel wanted to put her sons through college.

Born in 1927, Fertel was an exceptional student with a strong work ethic. She graduated from high school at 15 and worked part-time jobs while studying for a science degree at college. She began working as a teacher but quit in the late 1940s to marry and start a family.

Ten years later, however, the marriage ended, and when the alimony payments and a side-hustle making drapes at home didn't cover the bills, Fertel went back out to work as a lab assistant. By 1965, her two sons were teenagers and she realized that if they were to have the same education she had benefited from, then she was going to need to earn more money.

At first, she looked for extra work in bars and gas stations, but that just didn't suit her. Then she saw in the local paper that Chris' Steak House, a local restaurant, was up for sale.

The restaurant had failed numerous times under its then-owner, Chris Matulich, and Fertel had zero experience in the restaurant business. What's more, Matulich wanted $18,000 for the restaurant (equivalent to $180,000 today), and Fertel could only find that kind of money by mortgaging her house, which her banker, accountant, and best friend all urged her not to do. It's easy to understand their concern: she was so naïve about business that they had to explain that she needed to borrow more than $18,000 if she wanted to buy food to sell.[27]

At this point, few would have blamed Fertel for shrugging and saying, "Yeah, it's a nice idea, but I'm not sure I can do it." But she didn't. She borrowed $22,000 against her house and took on Chris' Steak House. Her mind was made up when she discovered that the restaurant had first opened on the day she was born. She took it as a sign that everything would work out.[28]

On the opening day, Fertel sold 35 steaks at $5 apiece. Within six months, she'd taken double what she'd been earning annually as a lab tech. She famously got involved in every aspect of the business—learning to saw 30-pound joints herself, hosting, helping the waitresses, keeping her own books—and she survived this heavy workload by napping on a mattress in a back room between serving hours.[29]

She also became known for employing many female single mothers, as she both identified with them and felt that they were reliable workers who deserved a chance. For many years, Chris' was the only New Orleans restaurant with an all-female waiting staff.[30]

There were many more twists and turns, but by the time Fertel passed away in 2002, she had built a nationwide steakhouse franchise, won various awards and accolades, and been dubbed the First Lady of Steak—a testament to her work ethic and ability to follow her heart and say, "Yeah, I'm not sure I can do it, *but...*"

REMEMBERING YOUR PURPOSE

Regardless of what others do, don't, may, or may not think, one crucial thing to bear in mind if this Yeah, But is holding you back is your purpose—your why.

Why did you want to embark on this project or pitch this idea in the first place? Do you feel it needs doing or has a purpose to fulfill? Is it something that has been overlooked or that could make a difference? Is it more important than the judgment of others? Will it affect people's lives for the better? Just as importantly, what will happen if it's *not* accomplished? How would that affect others, and how would it affect people's perception of you? Either way, your choice will have an impact and make ripples.

It's all about perception and priorities. And weighed against each other, how you perceive the importance of why you're doing something can make taking action appear far more positive and energizing than the fear of what others *might* say if you don't do it or if you try and fail.

BUT BUSTERS

Have you truly explored and understood the skills, resources, and support available to help you achieve your goal?

_____
_____
_____
_____
_____
_____

What's the worst that could happen if you try and fail? How can you mitigate those risks?

_____
_____
_____
_____
_____
_____

What past experiences or accomplishments can you draw strength from to remind yourself of your capabilities?

_____
_____
_____
_____
_____
_____

Are you allowing negative self-talk or external opinions to undermine your belief in yourself?

___

What's the potential cost of inaction or not even trying in the first place?

___

What's the first step you plan to take now that you've read this chapter?

___

Congratulations! You've started busting this Yeah, But!

YEAH, BUT… IT'S NOT SAFE

8

You're right. It isn't safe. Not completely. Almost nothing in life is. Hopping in an Uber? You're getting in a car with a complete stranger, trusting them to get you safely to your destination. Taking your car to the mechanic or calling an electrician to your house? How do you know that they'll do a thorough and competent job? Is it just based on reading reviews by other people—again, probably complete strangers you've never met?

Even the most trusted people, products, and companies can fail us, sometimes with disastrous consequences. Take Samsung's Galaxy Note 7 smartphone. It was launched in August 2016 but was recalled within a month because flaws in the battery design and manufacturing process caused a worrying number of devices to overheat, catch fire, and even explode.[31] Worse still, some of the replacement phones they issued were little better, causing airplanes to be evacuated and even hospitalizing users.

I'm not trying to cause consumer consumption panic. My point is that despite incidents like this, almost all of us still own a cell phone, and although Samsung's reputation suffered as a result of the Note 7 saga, millions of people still use their products today. Why? Because they weigh up the risk and say that what happened with one make of phone most likely won't happen with theirs. Risk doesn't necessarily mandate avoidance.

I like perspective, and you're going to read that word a lot here because the key to busting this particular Yeah, But is to put things into a rational perspective. It's about pausing and saying, "Okay, what are the realistic chances of my worst fears being realized here? What are the odds?"

A perceived lack of safety can come from different angles. You might convince yourself that something isn't safe, or other people might try to convince you that something isn't safe.

> **"If you can prove it, then move it."**
>
> – **Wolfe**ism

RISKY OR RECKLESS?

Of course, there are times when things truly aren't safe. You wouldn't cross the street without looking first or post your social security number online, but we're not talking about reckless behavior here. We're talking about the times when achieving your goal involves taking a risk, a leap of faith.

For example, if you wanted to set up a business or develop a product, you might need to take out a business loan or borrow funds. This obviously involves a level of risk because there's no certainty that your venture will work out as planned, if at all. The loan might be secured against your house, raising the stakes even higher.

The part of your brain that works to keep you safe might start trying to talk you out of taking such a big risk. Those around you might tell you the same thing—"Don't do it! It's not safe!"—and it's at this point that you have to start building and fortifying your rational perspective.

Remember that nothing in life is totally risk-free—you might give yourself a paper cut when you turn this page! So we have to start from that point and start weighing possibilities against each other. Is short-term borrowing worth the potential long-term gains?

We have to remain rational and reasonable when doing this, of course. Is spending every dollar you have on lottery tickets worth the potential gain of winning a million-dollar jackpot? That would be no–the odds are too high. But there are times in life when we have to be willing to take calculated risks. We need to evaluate the risk versus the short- and long-term rewards. We have to be confident enough to present ideas that people might not immediately like or are yet to understand. We have to speak up and share our thoughts.

A NATION OF RISK-TAKERS

Many people are "successful" by society's traditional definition–well-paid corporate job, nice house, family, the American dream–but they still feel stuck and sense their lives have gotten bland. Things are too safe. Despite their material prosperity, they're not satisfied. And they're not satisfied because they're not fulfilled. They could be 21, 65, or anywhere in between.

We often read inspirational stories where such people have walked away from their high-flying corporate careers to do something totally different. And the guiding principle is almost always an innate desire to achieve something that brings that mental fulfillment, even if the material rewards are less than what they've been accustomed to.

Of course, this often involves risk, and it might not always work out, but for them, the sense of moving forward in the direction they desire is worth the risk. The potential overall gains are worth the possible losses.

It's not always as dramatic as walking away from Wall Street to go work on a farm in Texas, but it is something many people do. The old ideas of a "job for life" no longer apply. That's partly because of how the world of work has changed but also because, as human beings, we're increasingly unlikely to stay in a career that doesn't fulfill us. We're more likely than ever to take a chance and try something else. If you're not convinced, then consider the statistics:

- A recent study indicated that over 49% of American workers were actively searching for new jobs.[32] Ongoing data suggests this trend may continue.
- A high percentage of older workers, around 80%, successfully transition to new careers after 45 years old.[33]

We can see that wanting to change your job is more common than not and that it's never too late to change paths—another statistic reveals that 39 is the average age at which Americans make a career change.[34]

On average, American workers can expect to hold around 12 jobs throughout their careers, with a typical job tenure lasting a little over four years.[35] When you look at it this way, you can see that the only constant is change. Things will alter far more than they stay the same, and with those changes comes the risk that things won't work out. But is that reason enough not to do it in the first place?

IS IT RISKIER TO PLAY IT SAFE?

Now let's look at this Yeah, But from a different direction. Okay, so something might involve a risk—maybe even a big risk that involves putting a lot on the line—but how does it compare to the risk involved in *not* taking that risk at all? What would happen if you played it totally safe and did nothing, changed nothing?

Sometimes, when you think about it, you can find that there's more danger in *not* taking action. You can miss out on opportunities. Others will beat you to the punch. The ship will sail, and you'll be left behind. Do you really want to stay doing what you're doing now for the rest of your days? Even if it's well-paid, the hours are good, and you don't hate your coworkers, is that really enough for this one life you have? Is that really the best use of the 1,440 minutes you're gifted every day?

And it's not just you that you have to think about. None of us exists in a vacuum. Our lives overlap with those of others, often more so than we realize. When I talk to a lot of my corporate leadership clients about what they want to achieve, they usually give me some variation of, "Oh, I just want to help others." That's wonderful and commendable, but it's also very broad. Sometimes, the people who say it also aren't willing to help themselves first. They won't take the kinds of risks that would enable them to advance to a stage where they genuinely could have a positive impact on the lives of others.

To get past this, as well as getting specific about *how* you want to help others, you can turn your basic desire to help into a strong, motivating perspective. Ask yourself what's at stake in terms of your potential impact. Start thinking about whose lives are going to be negatively affected if you *don't* see this thing through. Who could have benefited from your idea, your words, or your project but will not because you did not want to risk taking that crucial step?

WHAT IF?

Another great tactic for getting around this Yeah, But is to externalize all the ways in which you think doing a certain thing isn't "safe." Is it not safe because you might lose money? You might lose face? You'll feel embarrassed if things don't work out? You won't get to lead other projects? The list goes on. (See *Yeah, But... What Will Others Say or Think?*)

Get real with yourself. Write down what it is you want to do. Then write down all of the risks involved. You don't have to show them to anyone, but it's important that you write them down rather than just think about them. Why? Because I guarantee that the list will look different on a piece of paper in front of you than it did in your head.

Remember when you were a kid, lying in bed at night? How silhouettes in your room could start looking more and more scary until you turned on the light and saw that it was just the way your belongings were arranged? Well, doing this task is like that. You freeze your fear of the irrational unknown by bringing it into the rational known. You shine a light on your thought process and assess whether the risks are a) all that dangerous and b) realistically going to happen.

What's more, you can plan how to respond should any of the risks you've itemized happen. You can better prepare yourself. This might take the form of a Plan B—what alternate course of action you'll take—or it could be what you will gain or learn from having gone out there and taken the risk. This could be anything from new connections made in the process to simply the experience of having tried to succeed.

YOU TAKE MORE RISKS THAN YOU REALIZE

Here's the thing: you're already a risk-taker. Throughout this chapter, we've seen there are risks everywhere, from career changes to exploding cell phones. Thousands of cyclists are injured and even killed on the roads each year. So are vehicle drivers and pedestrians. But that likely doesn't stop you from walking, driving, or cycling. You probably never even consider the risks before you embark on a journey.

Instead, you work from a far more rational perspective, even if you don't realize you're doing it. You start your journey and assess and manage risks as you go. Most drivers don't avoid the highway because a speeding car might crash into them. They drive on the roads and do what they need to do to drive safely and avoid any potential harm.

In other words, yes, there is a risk in almost everything, but the healthiest perspective is not avoidance or hurling yourself into something without taking any precautions. It lies in the middle instead. If you feel that reaching your destination can be achieved without catastrophe, the healthiest perspective is to at least start moving, ensuring you remain agile enough on the way and avoid unnecessary risks.

10 MINUTES FROM NOW...

Author Suzy Welch has an excellent system for helping us gain perspective. It's called the 10-10-10 rule,[36] from her book of the same name, and it's designed to help with decision-making.

The first step is the 10-minute perspective. This is what you're feeling right *now*. The immediacy and the burden, the excitement and the anxiety. It can feel overwhelming, but it's transient. It will pass. Then, you consider the second step: the 10-month perspective. If this is a big dream or goal, then 10 months from now is when you'll likely be in the middle of it, when things are really daunting. That too will pass. So you then consider the 10-year perspective, when you're down the road and looking back. What do you see?

Here's an example of this from my youth: I worked in a restaurant for a while because I wanted to earn enough to buy a car. My 10-minute perspective wasn't great. But I lived with it. I knew that 10 months down the line, I'd still likely be working in a pancake restaurant. I didn't know if I'd be enjoying it by then, or how much batter I'd be covered in, but I judged that my goal of being able to afford my first car would make it worthwhile.

My 10-year perspective was different. I knew for sure that I would not still be working in the food industry a decade later, let alone working in that restaurant. I knew that I wanted to be an entrepreneur and own my own business and this was only a job and not a career. That totally altered my perspective, how I approached the job, and how I saw myself. As long as I stayed focused on my 10-10-10, I could stay focused on what I wanted to achieve without getting trapped.

So when you do this, everything suddenly changes because you are assessing your risks rationally and looking at things in terms of gain, not loss. You're balancing reasonable caution with an optimistic growth mindset.

BUT BUSTERS

How can you shift your perspective from focusing solely on risks to considering the potential gains and opportunities that come with taking calculated chances?

___

___

___

___

___

___

Reflecting on past experiences, what are some instances where you took risks that led to positive outcomes, and how can you apply those lessons to current situations where you're hesitant to take risks?

___

___

___

___

___

___

In what ways can you differentiate between true danger and perceived risk in order to make more informed decisions about pursuing your goals and dreams?

___

How might externalizing your concerns and fears by writing them down help you gain clarity and develop actionable plans to mitigate risks and pursue your aspirations?

___

What is your 10-10-10 right now? And how does getting this perspective influence your decision-making process?

___

What's the first step you plan to take now that you've read this chapter?

_____
_____
_____

Congratulations! You've started busting this Yeah, But!

YEAH, BUT… I NEED HELP!

9

One of the biggest potential roadblocks to completing and achieving your goals is getting stuck in a rut. It's so easy to fall into routines and habits that don't move you forward. Sometimes, it can feel like you're grinding away, doing the same thing over and over and never getting anywhere, like a wheel stuck in the mud, spinning and spinning to no avail. Other times, it can even feel like quite a nice rut. You still don't get anywhere, but things are always so-so. Everything is just okay. You have the security of knowing your redundant routine inside out, yet all the while you still know you're stuck there.

This doesn't just happen to us as individuals. It can infect whole teams and organizations, too. Think of anyone—companies, brands, sports teams, entertainers—that lost their dominance because they kept doing the same thing over and over again to the point where they were just going through the motions. It might have worked at one point, but now it's just bland, boring, or has been superseded to the point where competitors have figured out their game plan.

GETTING UNSTUCK

To start tackling this Yeah, But, let's take a step back. When do we need help? It's when we're stuck. But how can we recognize that we need help if we don't know we're stuck? Sometimes we can be so busy, so focused on anything that feels like motion, like keeping those wheels spinning in the mud, that we don't even realize that we're stuck—or we don't want to admit that we are.

Equally, if we're stuck in a nice, safe, secure little rut, it's easy to let the days, weeks, months, and even years pass by. We keep thinking, "I'll change things tomorrow, next week, whenever." The Spanish have a word for the indefinite future: *mañana*. And that's where most of our plans can end up getting stuck, in a kind of future limbo. Things will change *mañana*.

But as I discuss in *Yeah, But... I Don't Have Time*, you've got 1,440 minutes in each day that you're not getting back. However you've gotten stuck, it's important to realize that it's happened and that you might need a hand to help you out of it.

EVEN THE BEST NEED HELP SOMETIMES

Now sometimes, especially if we don't want to admit that we're stuck, we can become like the driver who refuses to admit they're lost but won't pull over to ask for directions and ends up getting more and more frustrated and embarrassed—not to mention more and more lost.

The thing to stress here is that, far too often, we likely know on some level that we need help. It can be for many different reasons. We might not know what to do next (if so, see *Yeah, But... I Don't Know What to Do Next*). We might be doing things that *should* be working but aren't, and we can't figure out why. Or we might just not be able to achieve our goals alone. But whatever our reason, we see asking for help as a sign of weakness, even of failure.

The reasons for this are partly due to pride and partly because of society. We see the likes of Jeff Bezos, Sheryl Sandberg, Elon Musk, Warren Buffett, etc., and we perceive strong and determined individuals who reached the top all by themselves.

The American dream of pulling yourself up by your bootstraps has become almost literal. It's you and you alone against the world. Anything less doesn't count because it shows fragility.

But right away, we can dismantle that. Not only is it false, but it's also impossible. No one is an island. Success is never a one-person show, and no one has the answer to everything. We all have our limits and our blind spots: you, me, and the richest person in the world. There is not one successful person on this planet from any walk of life who succeeded alone. Everyone had to learn something from someone else. They needed a support network. They relied on others' financial resources, someone to open doors for them, a champion, a great teacher or trainer, and a team of experts around them to help them move things forward. They required others in their corner.

Let's think about Jamaican Olympic star Usain Bolt. Did he become the world's greatest sprinter on his own? Did he fund his own training and go off to the track every day by himself, timing his own runs and devising his own diet and training program? Of course not. Yes, he won races and gold medals because he could reach the finish line faster than everyone else, but he also had a great team around him to get him to the starting line in the best possible shape to succeed. He had a lot of help. In that sense, could we say that successful individuals are the outcome of a team process?

CASE STUDY: NORMAN WOODLAND AND THE POWER OF SHARING IDEAS

Barcodes have been such a ubiquitous part of product packaging for so long that it's hard to imagine a time when they didn't exist and shop assistants had to remember or look up the price of every item and then type it into a clunky old cash register. It's estimated that 5 billion barcodes are now scanned every day, so that's a lot of memory and data entry saved!

Norman Woodland was one of the co-creators of the barcode.[37] Back in the late 1940s, his classmate at what is now Drexel University, Bernard Silver, told him about a conversation he'd overheard between a supermarket executive and Drexel's dean of engineering. The executive had asked the dean for help devising a way to automate the logging of product information, as the existing system was too slow and labor intensive.

The dean had turned down the request, but Silver told Woodland about it, stirring his interest. Inspiration came to Woodland when he was sitting on a beach, drawing lines in the sand. He realized that lines could be used like the dots and dashes of Morse code—thin lines and larger lines. The basic idea of the barcode was born.

Utilizing the power of collaboration, Woodland worked with Silver to develop the idea, and in 1949, they applied for a patent for the first barcode, which was eventually granted in 1952.

But there was still a long way to go. Woodland had known he needed Silver's help to develop his initial idea, and he also knew that to be properly implemented, the idea would need further development and investment from an established technology company.

Woodland had started working for IBM in 1951, and he'd tried to sell the patent to them, hoping to work on developing it with them. IBM's offer was too low, however, and Woodland and Silver eventually sold it to an electronics company called Philco in 1962. They later sold it on to RCA, and finally, in Ohio in 1974, the first barcode was used in a supermarket. Woodland's initial idea had taken some 25 years to answer the problem it was created to solve.

At almost every vital stage of the creative process, Woodland recognized that he needed the help of others. He could have tried to charge forward, jealously guarding his revolutionary concept, but he didn't. He worked with his colleague to perfect the patented idea and then sought the backing of a larger company. When that didn't work out as he'd hoped, he sold it elsewhere. In fact, it's arguable that the only time he and Silver should have asked for help was in negotiating a better selling price, as they reportedly accepted an offer of just $15,000 ($156,000 in 2025). Not much to show for such a life-changing idea!

CASE STUDY: IGNAZ SEMMELWEIS AND WHY BRILLIANCE ALONE IS NOT ENOUGH

In *Yeah, But… I Don't Have Time*, we met Ignaz Semmelweis, the 19th-century physician who became an advocate of doctors washing their hands between tasks to help prevent mothers and their newborn children from catching infections and dying. We also noted that such hygienic practices didn't become the norm until after Semmelweis had died. One reason for this is that doctors resisted adopting Semmelweis' ideas because, they claimed, they didn't have time. This is partly true, but more recent research has also placed some of the blame on Semmelweis himself.

Today, it's argued that another reason Semmelweis' ideas about hygiene didn't catch on was a language barrier. Although he was working in Vienna, Austria, a hub of medical excellence, Semmelweis came from neighboring Hungary. He never mastered the German language of his colleagues enough to properly convey his findings to them. What's more, he took too long to publish and publicize his research. By the time he did, he was no longer working in Vienna. The optimal moment had passed.

There's an important subtlety here for us. Semmelweis' language problems could arguably have been solved had he asked for help. He also might have been able to publicize his findings more effectively. What he did instead was largely pass responsibility for the latter to others without properly explaining vital intricacies in his findings. The result was that the most important aspects of his research were missed in his lifetime. Mothers and children kept dying unnecessarily, and Semmelweis became bitter and paranoid.

You could say that this unhappy state of affairs was because Semmelweis passed the buck, which is not the same as asking for help. It also highlights that when you do ask for help, it's critical to articulate exactly what it is you want help with. If you don't, you might find that the help you asked for is no help at all.

> *"There are three main options in addressing change: IGNORE it, INVESTIGATE it, or IMPLEMENT it. Choose wisely."*
>
> *- **Wolfe**ism*

COGNITIVE DIVERSITY

It follows that once we've realized and admitted that we need help—and that it's okay to ask for help—the logical next step is to go about getting it. And this means asking others for their input and advice.

As people, we have a deep-seated need for connection and belonging. Throughout history, we've thrived in groups, relying on each other for support, safety, and shared experiences. This natural tendency to form close bonds with others is a core part of who we are. The rise of social media hasn't helped. It's easier than ever for us to get unintentionally siloed with people who appear to share the same values, beliefs, likes, and dislikes as us. But what does that do for our perspective? How does it help us get unstuck if we only engage with people who think as we do? We would be prone to coming up with similar ideas.

Engaging with different perspectives, meanwhile, can be hugely transformative. Plenty of research has been done, including a *Harvard Business Review* report entitled 'Why Diverse Teams Are Smarter,'[38] showing that the dynamics of more diverse teams can lead to better decision-making and stronger outcomes. Why? Because groups of people who approach the same problem from different directions and are encouraged to respectfully disagree are more likely to find creative ways past roadblocks.

Obviously, team members' skills have to be strong and complementary to succeed. If they're not, then it's diversity for its own sake, which is self-defeating, but the right balance of different views can offer you a much wider scope and challenge you to look at problems in a new way.

ACCEPTING CHANGE

If you're stuck in a rut or just plain stuck, then is fear of change one of the things that's holding you back? Even in unproductive situations, it's easy to get used to, and maybe even comfortable with, things being the way they are. If you believe, however subconsciously, that the only worthwhile success is that which is hard-earned, then maybe you're afraid of getting unstuck because you define yourself by the fight to succeed? If you were to win that fight, then you'd have to surrender that part of your identity. In other words, you'd lose the thrill of the chase.

As we saw earlier, ego and pride can play their part too. But if we never change, and if we're never challenged to change, then we end up unquestioningly accepting the same old dysfunctional status quo. We also end up being overtaken by those who are nimbler and more adaptable.

Sometimes, achieving a goal can mean much broader changes. One that is fairly common is letting go of unhealthy relationships that don't serve you or your purpose and finding a new "pack" to run with and get help from.

We can turn to learning a new language as an example of this. Let's say you want to become fluent in Italian. It might be for travel purposes, or it might just be to challenge yourself intellectually. Mastering a new language requires consistent practice and dedication. You can't simply travel to an Italian-speaking country and expect to converse fluently without putting in the effort beforehand.

Some of your friends might resist the idea, especially if they aren't interested in expanding their horizons or have their own Yeah, Buts. You might hear things like, "Why bother learning a new language when everyone speaks English anyway?" They might try to tempt you with other activities or discourage you from spending time studying. However, as you immerse yourself in learning, you'll find support from friends who share your enthusiasm or discover language exchange groups where you can connect with others who encourage and assist you in your journey. In the end, you surpass your initial limitations and break free from restrictive mindsets and relationships.

A similar thing is true in business, even when it seems that you're going it alone. Let's say you start up a business by yourself as a solopreneur. The business grows, and you take on staff, but ultimately, you are the only "founder" there. Those around you are all your employees or contractors. They won't necessarily share your goals or values. They might not be qualified or even interested in helping you navigate roadblocks and struggles as they occur. But if you reach out beyond your office walls, you'll find local business networks where there are others in the same situation.

MENTORS AND ADVISORS

Another way of obtaining the right kind of support is to get a mentor or advisor. They sound very similar, but their roles are subtly different.

Mentors can be casual or formal. I had a great casual mentor when I was first starting out. He was one of my first bosses, and although he was never a personal friend, he cared about me while keeping an objective eye on my future. He would challenge me with business opportunities and introductions and start conversations about life-oriented goals. All these years later, I still reflect on those discussions we had and the leaders he helped me meet.

You might find a similar casual mentor among your peer group; someone you can go to periodically who will consistently offer objective help and advice that enables you to stay focused.

Professional mentors are more formal. You engage them to help you move toward achieving a specific goal. You own the process and the results, but they are there to hold you accountable and offer advice along the way, helping you to develop your skills and mindset and choose the best path forward based on your situation.

Conversely, advisors are usually professionals in their field who offer advice and nothing else. They're not invested in any wider aspects of your personal development. In other words, let's say you wanted to know the answer to a math problem. An advisor would tell you the answer. A mentor would help you in a way whereby you could work out the solution for yourself.

You can even employ combined mentors and advisors, a powerful combination that helps you develop both professionally and personally.

BUT BUSTERS

Who do you know with more experience or expertise in your area of interest who can counsel you on your journey?

_____

_____

_____

_____

_____

What does assistance look like? Define what you need and when it would be beneficial. Support comes in many ways. Determine whether it's a book, training, a long-term mentor, or a short burst of inspired answers.

_____

_____

_____

_____

_____

In what ways can you challenge the misconception that asking for help is a sign of weakness or failure, especially in a society that often glorifies individual success? How can you redefine success to include collaboration and seeking assistance when needed?

_____

_____

_____

_____

_____

_____

If you're already getting help and assistance from others, can they offer a diverse range of perspectives? Or do they all think like you?

_____

_____

_____

_____

_____

How can you overcome the fear of change and the comfort of maintaining the status quo, especially when it may require letting go of identities or relationships that no longer serve your goals?

_____

_____

_____

_____

_____

What's the first step you plan to take now that you've read this chapter?

_____

_____

_____

Congratulations! You've started busting this Yeah, But!

COLLEAGUE CASE STUDY:
MARC DEDMAN– NAVIGATING YOUR OWN YEAH, BUTS AND THOSE OF OTHERS

Marc Dedman is a friend and colleague whom I've known for many years. Like the others I've written about in this book, he'd achieved a level of success that would satisfy many people: he was a senior attorney at a multistate law firm, a role he'd held for some time. He'd done well for himself, personally and professionally. He had a strong reputation in his field, he was financially secure, and he had a happy, loving family around him. What more could anyone want?

A few years back, however, I helped Marc when, through our chats over coffee, he explained that he was trying to work through a difficult professional and personal analysis. He'd wisely noticed that the specific area in which his firm specialized was going to become unsustainable in the long term. He foresaw that there were going to be more and more firms chasing fewer and fewer contracts. Even established firms like his couldn't afford to rest on their laurels.

Marc believed that he knew the path the firm should take. He wanted them to expand into another potentially lucrative area of law. But that required a lot of commitment from a lot of stakeholders. Not only would it need significant time and investment on the firm's part, but it would also involve them being prepared to take a risk, as success was by no means guaranteed.

On top of that, Marc also had his own Yeah, Buts to overcome. He was, by this time, a fair way into his career, and he was a family man with long-term financial commitments. If the risk didn't pay off, it would affect his wife and children as well as his professional reputation. At the same time, standing still and letting his Yeah, Buts win out might have the same effect. Either way, he knew that inaction was not an option. A decision had to be made, and the results would probably be life-changing whichever path he chose. He invited me to help him navigate this difficult scenario.

While I never formally coached Marc, I was intrigued by his situation, as I could see he was facing a dilemma. Also, he's a friend, and so I obviously wanted to use my experience to help him as best I could. I recently spoke to him about his memories of that period and how, with sharing my perspective, he navigated his way through. "At the time, the firm I worked for was very successful, but I felt like we were reaching the point where we wouldn't be able to grow any further," he recalled. "Not only that, but the way I saw things, our market was only going to start shrinking. Contracts were going to reach their natural end, and new ones were going to become harder to find. I had this idea for expanding into a new practice area that I believed could generate significant revenue and diversify our services."

Unfortunately, the people who mattered—Marc's partners in the firm—didn't see what he saw. "They weren't on board with it," he says. "They saw it as too risky an investment because that kind of expansion would have needed some serious time and money behind it."

Herein lies a challenge: navigating other people's Yeah, Buts as well as one's own. Despite Marc's experience, knowledge, and reputation, his peers still said, "Yeah, but it's not safe." They weren't telling him that he was wrong or that his ideas were bad; they just weren't prepared to take the leap of faith necessary (we talk more about such uncertainties in *Yeah, But... It's Not Safe*).

And try as Marc might, he couldn't get them to move past their Yeah, But. And sometimes, tough though it can be to accept, you can't solve others' problems for them.

Although Marc was passionate about his plan and convinced that it was both workable and profitable, he was also battling his own Yeah, Buts. His age was a factor, not because he didn't feel capable but because, by that point in his life, he'd not only built a stable and successful career but also a home and a family. He had a wife; he had a son and daughter he was helping to put through college and law school respectively. He wasn't a hungry 20-something with few ties or commitments and everything to prove. He had everything to lose.

Marc and I would meet up for coffee and have impactful conversations about where he was at and what potentially lay ahead. "Those conversations you and I had helped me realize that I had the experience and knowledge to do this," he recalls today. "I'd already helped establish my firm's presence, both state-wide and across state lines before."

The way I helped Marc realize his potential was to help him break everything down into smaller pieces and appraise them as practically as possible. Was there any more information out there that could help him with this? If so, where could he get it? I encouraged him to think about the potential for success and the opportunities that could increase that potential.

Ultimately, Marc decided to go for it in a big way. The tipping point came when he asked his wife, "Would you rather me lay on my deathbed wondering what would have happened with my idea, or would you rather me think about you and our family?" It was a strong way of putting it, but his wife gave him her backing.

Shortly after that, Marc reached out to a law firm in another state and proposed that he open an office for them in his jurisdiction. It was a bold move, but it paid off better than Marc could have imagined. Events moved quickly. Within months, the new firm opened their first office in Marc's home state, working in the area that he'd proposed to his former partners. The concept proved so successful that the office grew as large as the one Marc had left. He brought in new clients and tempted others from his old firm. Poignantly, these clients would have stayed with Marc's old firm had the partners been willing to say, "Yeah, but let's take a chance."

"The whole experience taught me that Yeah, Buts can be multifaceted and involve many parties," Marc says, looking back. "But ultimately, we can only act on those Yeah, Buts that we control. I couldn't solve my old firm's Yeah, Buts for them if they weren't willing to meet halfway. So for me, it was about weighing everything up, deciding to take that calculated risk and making a significant change when it mattered most.

And that is the essence of overcoming Yeah, Buts. You can't always control every aspect or change other people's minds, but when you decide to own what you can control, when you realize that the time is right for positive action, then you can move to where you're meant to be.

YEAH, BUT… I'M TOO OLD OR TOO YOUNG 10

Whenever a client says, "Yeah, but I'm too old" or "Yeah, but I'm too young," the first thing I say is, "Tell me more."

Why? Because I know that, within minutes, they'll be giving justifications based on what they see around them. They've almost always convinced themselves that they're too old or too young because they think that's what society believes.

It's true that there are barriers in society that exclude people based solely on their age. The most obvious is ageism—the false belief that creativity, innovation, and even basic competence are only for the young. It's as if you wake up on a certain birthday—your 30th or 40th, for example—and are now "old." You can't do any of the things you could do 24 hours ago when you were still "young."

But there are also more general societal expectations and unwritten rules that people in certain age groups should only do certain things. The young can feel pressured into knowing what they want to do. Those in their thirties, particularly women, can feel pressured into "settling down" and having kids—their "biological clock is ticking." Those above a certain age, meanwhile, should be thinking about retiring, downsizing, and slowing down. *Really?*

Sometimes, these pressures might be heaped on us by others. Other times, we might subconsciously put them upon ourselves based on constant messaging that we've internalized and allowed to become an inner narrative. We feel we *should* have hit certain targets by certain dates or ages, whether we want to hit them or not. There can also be a lack of positive role models, too. If we see someone in their seventies doing things supposedly meant for younger people, it tends to be presented as a novelty or even a joke. The same goes for teenage entrepreneurs and young politicians. There's often a subtly patronizing tone to the articles and accompanying comments.

I get that sometimes there are factual barriers to what can be achieved at certain ages, but most of my clients—and I work with people aged anywhere from 19 to 79—who have experienced this Yeah, But have encountered no such barriers. When they first come to me, what we soon discover is that they've believed the bias. They stop and get stuck before achieving their goal. However, as we work through this Yeah, But together, they quickly come to realize that there's rarely a basis for their belief that they're too young or old.

So how do we start reframing this belief here and now? Well, it's important to remember that even when there are real barriers, internal or external, almost nothing is 100% true for 100% of people 100% of the time. There's almost always an exception somewhere. Someone somewhere has bucked the trend. What if you were in the percentage, however small, that *didn't* experience the barrier? Even if you did, what if you were able to overcome it, work around it, or at least minimize its effects?

If you're stuck on this Yeah, But because you've believed or created a narrative around something you haven't directly experienced, it's important to challenge that narrative by looking for exceptions to the rule. They're often a great source of inspiration for helping you overcome it.

DOES AGE DEFINE YOU? OR DO YOUR TALENTS DEFINE YOU?

One of the many great guests I've had on my *The Yeah, But Podcast* is Bonnie Stith, who worked for the US Central Intelligence Agency (CIA) for over 30 years. She joined the Agency when she was just 22 years old, and this inevitably brought a lot of judgment from more senior colleagues about her age versus their conventional wisdom. "I was at the very young end of the people coming in," she explained to me. "So I was always 'too young.' And I would hear that: 'Yeah, but you're too young,' or 'Once you're older, you'll understand this.' Constantly being judged about my age created a certain dynamic where I felt like I had to be tougher. In fact, I was told by a senior officer that I had better develop a thick skin. [I] believed the narrative that was often repeated to me and had to toughen up and act older. I think I've always been a little bit of an old soul, [but] I had to act even older."

Stith didn't let others labeling her with this Yeah, But hold her back. If anything, by her own admission, it toughened her up and made her even more determined to prove herself. Conversely, by the time she'd achieved a senior position as a Director of the Center for Cyber Intelligence for the CIA, she began running into the opposite Yeah, But. "You get in the mindset of… anything over 50 is too old," she explained, "because many of my role models and peers were retiring when they turned 50. Once we had determined that we were making a career of our time at the Agency, we started planning for what we would do when we retired at 50. At the age of 22, 50 seemed so old! Then I found myself at 50 and realized I still had so much to give!"

Again, Stith could have let this Yeah, But confine her. She'd reached a grade in the CIA where she could have worked past the service's mandatory retirement age, staying comfortable and reasoning that she was too old to learn new tricks. But she didn't. She retired and retrained as a credentialed leadership coach, mentor coach, and coach supervisor. Today, she runs a thriving coaching and consulting business.

CASE STUDY: ALAN RICKMAN—A DESIGN FOR LIFE?

One of the most famous examples of someone who initially thought, "Yeah, but I'm too old" but eventually proved himself wrong is the late British actor Alan Rickman.

Rickman was born in London in 1946. He graduated from art college in the mid-1960s and began working as a successful graphic designer, even launching an agency that worked on album art for rock bands. In his spare time, he also performed with an amateur dramatics company. By his mid-twenties, friends were telling him that he should audition for RADA (Royal Academy of Dramatic Art), London's premier acting school, but he initially believed he was too old.

Deep down, however, he knew that acting was what he wanted to do. His design business was successful, but he felt that a life spent in graphic design would become overly repetitive. He later reflected that an inner voice told him that it was "now or never" to make the leap into acting. So, in 1972, at age 26, he wrote to RADA, asking for an audition. He was accepted and spent two years there, making his professional stage debut at age 28.[39]

Rickman remained semi-professional for several years after graduation, acting in the theater and occasionally on British television until 1985, when, in his late thirties, he co-starred in a stage production of *Les Liaisons Dangereuses*, which eventually transferred from the West End to Broadway and won him a coveted Tony Award. In 1988, he made his feature film debut in *Die Hard* alongside Bruce Willis. Now in his early forties, he had finally arrived in Hollywood, and for the rest of his life, he would be one of the most acclaimed and sought-after British actors on both sides of the Atlantic.[40]

CASE STUDY: SUSAN BOYLE—SHE DREAMED A DREAM, THEN LIVED IT

If Alan Rickman's story is one of overcoming the belief that you're too old, then the story of a fellow Brit, Susan Boyle, is one of overcoming *others'* belief that you're too old.

Boyle was 47 years old in 2009 when she auditioned for an episode of *Britain's Got Talent*. As she first walked out onstage, everyone from the judges to the audience raised their eyebrows and audibly stifled laughter at the sight of this greying, middle-aged, unemployed woman from a small Scottish town announcing that she wanted to be a singing star. She told the show's hosts that she'd never been given the chance to perform to such a large crowd before, generally because of her looks and, more recently, her age. In fact, like Alan Rickman, she'd needed some persuasion to be there. She'd gotten cold feet over appearing on the show and started thinking that maybe she *was* too old after all.

But her audition song, 'I Dreamed a Dream' from *Les Miserables*, left the crowd and the judges stunned. They had clearly thought that Boyle was the kind of deluded dreamer that they could all make fun of. After all, she didn't look the part, *and* she was far too old. 47-year-olds don't try to succeed in the highly competitive, youth-focused field of music and entertainment. And if they do, they generally make fools of themselves, right? But within seconds, they were cheering her on. They had no choice. She was that good.

Boyle's story has become legendary. By the end of 2009, she had topped the charts on both sides of the Atlantic with her debut album, which remains one of the biggest-selling records of the 21st century. Now in her early sixties, she continues to record and perform all over the world.[41]

MOVE THROUGH

So let's start looking at ways to move through this Yeah, But. Whether you feel you're the wrong age to accomplish something because it's what you believe or what society appears to be telling you, then either way, you're believing in a story. Additionally, it's likely a story that isn't based on your direct experience.

Once you recognize this, you can start looking at your age in a different light. So what if you're a certain age? Has someone your age achieved what you want to achieve before? And even if they haven't, is achieving it 100% impossible? If not, then the likelihood is that age isn't what's holding you back. It's your *beliefs* about your age. These can be stronger than you think. Someone as young as 30 might believe themselves "over the hill" because they're no longer in their twenties, and they will seem older because of it. Equally, someone in their fifties might have the vitality and optimism of a 21-year-old, but with the added bonus of extra life experience. Your age is *objective*. Your perspective on it is *subjective*.

You don't need to aim for the level of success and public recognition that Alan Rickman and Susan Boyle achieved to prove yourself or your doubters wrong, either. There might not even be anything to prove. These days, we are living and staying active for longer than ever before. Take a look at photographs of 60-somethings from, say, 30 or 40 years ago and compare them to 60-somethings today. The difference is incredible. People are staying younger for longer, and it's not just down to cosmetics or fashion. Age is simply becoming less relevant to how people feel about themselves and how they feel they must present themselves.

TURN IT AROUND

One thing you can do to turn this Yeah, But around is to say, "Okay, what wisdom do I possess?" If you're what we generally term "middle-aged" or "senior," think how much valuable experience that gives you to pull from. What perspectives can you offer that someone younger can't?

If you're in your late teens and feel patronized or not taken seriously, or if you feel that your youth makes you too inexperienced to accomplish something, then turn your age to your advantage by reflecting on its positive aspects. What fresh perspectives can you bring? Can you bring more energy to a project? Are you more open to trying and learning new things, even your use of technology? Are you more flexible with your time than someone who is older and maybe has family commitments?

Once you've looked at age in terms of gain rather than loss, then you're seeing yourself in a new light. And if you are older, it doesn't mean you can't still learn new skills. You can *always* learn, whatever your age. Yes, some skills may be more difficult than others, but they're not impossible. Equally, if you're younger, it doesn't automatically mean that you don't have valuable experience or insight. Remember, age is not a one-size-fits-all. We all grow and develop at different speeds with a unique combination of experiences. Our mindset has more say in whether we can or can't accomplish something than our age.

Ultimately, whether you're 18, 36, or 72 doesn't mean you will (or should) have achieved certain milestones or experienced certain things. You are you, and you can only be where you are right now with your one-off blend of learning and experience. The digits on your birth certificate have little bearing on what you can become going forward, as they only state how long you have been around.

BUT BUSTERS

How can you shift your perspective from viewing age as a limiting factor to recognizing it as merely one data point that, taken alone, doesn't define personal capabilities?

_____
_____
_____
_____
_____
_____

In what ways can you reframe your beliefs about age to empower yourself in pursuing your goals?

_____
_____
_____
_____
_____
_____

What strategies can you employ to overcome age-related doubts and pursue your aspirations?

_____
_____
_____
_____
_____
_____

How might you leverage the experiences and perspectives gained through aging to your advantage, irrespective of societal norms or expectations?

_____
_____
_____
_____
_____

When confronting doubts about age and its impact on achievement, what steps can you take to focus on personal strengths and potential rather than perceived limitations?

_____
_____
_____
_____
_____

What's the first step you plan to take now that you've read this chapter?

_____
_____
_____

Congratulations! You've started busting this Yeah, But!

YEAH, BUT... YOU CAN'T WHERE I COME FROM

11

Sometimes, we can come to believe that where we were born, where we grew up, where we first started, or how we first saw ourselves are definitive. This can sometimes be a positive thing—it can give us a deep sense of being rooted and of having somewhere to work from—but equally, it can sometimes feel like cement around our feet. It keeps us stuck. We feel unable to move, change, or better ourselves.

If the latter resonates with you, then the good news is that it doesn't have to be that way anymore. Your hometown and your class status have as much of a say in defining who you are as the part-time job you had in high school does.

You might come from a town, city, county, or even a state that isn't known for anything positive. Maybe it only tops polls of places with the worst crime rate, highest unemployment, or worst healthcare. It might be a blue-collar place known for manual labor. This is not a problem in itself, but the kinds of struggles that are common in such places—low wages, low expectations, etc.—can unhelpfully become seen as "just the way it is." It's a stifling attitude that can affect you to the core, even if you don't consciously realize it.

I know that kind of place and attitude too well because I grew up in such a town in northern New Jersey. In times gone by, the neighboring town had been known for its mills. It still had plenty of factories when I was a child, and the prevailing attitude was one of just "getting the job done," keeping your head down, and not making a fuss.

The common aim for most of my neighbors was to simply survive, which meant slogging away for the reward of getting to do it all over again the next day. There were too few success stories. There weren't abundant and willing mentors waiting to help you, and there were very few people to connect with on a higher level. You just stayed in your lane.

But even in a town where not rocking the boat was the order of the day, you could still find yourself being thrown overboard, and my family is, unfortunately, a prime example. My parents divorced when I was seven. They filed for bankruptcy, and our treasured, avocado-colored Plymouth Satellite 4-door sedan had been repossessed. I was kicked out of public school at age nine for being "too smart and disruptive", and my mom and I were living in an apartment, surviving on government benefits of Welfare and food stamps, subsidized milk, and government cheese.

At the time, this was just how things were. I didn't realize I'd grown up in poverty until years later when someone said, "Hey Marc, you were raised by a divorced mom who had multiple jobs, you lived in an apartment, and you came from a broken home." But I do get it. I understand how others who had such starts in life can internalize those attitudes and say things like, "It just doesn't happen for the likes of me" when they don't get the job or the lucky break. I get why they might not even consider trying to better themselves in the first place. It can feel like you're in a self-imposed prison. But I repeat that *it doesn't have to be that way anymore*. If this Yeah, But is yours, then remember that it's not an objective prison that you're in. It's only a notion. If you try the door, you'll find that it opens.

CASE STUDY: DEVON HARRIS' JOURNEY FROM FIREHOUSE TO THE WINTER OLYMPICS

"You can't find new lands if you don't lose sight of the shoreline."

– Devon Harris

The Jamaican bobsled team will perhaps forever be associated with the hit 1990s movie *Cool Runnings*. But behind that Hollywood fiction is a real story of someone who overcame this Yeah, But in grand style. His name is Devon Harris. He's a former captain in the Jamaican military, a three-time Olympian, and he now works as a motivational speaker here in the United States.[42]

I had the pleasure of interviewing Devon so that I could get his story. "I'm scared of speed and height," he told me. "And, of course, bobsledding is about speed and height. The speed part is obvious, but the height thing is more of a perception. When you're standing at the top of the track, and you can see the finish curve, you get this perception of a precipitous fall, although in reality, the track winds around the side of the mountain; it's not one straight run-down. But that doesn't matter. You *perceive* this height and this precipitous fall. So, my first time in a bobsled, I'm behind a guy who has never driven one before, and I'm scared to death. And I said to myself–I remember the moment–I just said, "If I die, I die." I also thought, "Could I die? Yeah. But I'm willing to take the chance. I'm gonna risk that because there's no way I'm going to come all this way and not go!" And what was kind of amazing about that evening was that we did three runs. And I remember on the third run, I was so scared, but I was excited as hell."

But it's not only the fact that someone from the Caribbean could compete in a winter sport that is significant here. It's that Devon came from what he calls "the hood"—Sunrise Drive in Kingston, sometimes known as "Firehouse" because of its reputation for violence. It would have been easy for him to stay there and say, "This is all there is," but he didn't. He joined the Jamaican military and even attended Sandhurst in Britain, the most prestigious military school in the world. By the time the bobsledding opportunity came along, he was already a commissioned army officer. He'd already overcome this Yeah, But once.

"I think back to when I was growing up, and I just hated being poor," he says. "I hated the limitations that my environment suggests. I didn't have a clear path [but] I just knew I had to do it (see *Yeah, But… What's the Plan?*). And that's the thing. I think most people get jammed up on figuring out exactly *how* they're going to do it. I know it's not necessarily the best advice for business persons, but I just think that instinctively, intuitively, you just have to know. You have to be willing to put yourself out there and be hugely uncomfortable, to feel like a fish out of water. And all of us actually have it within us—the potential and the ability to go from where we are to the next level. But we are not willing to be hugely uncomfortable."

Devon also readily agrees that where you're from cannot and should not hold you back. "Exactly," he says. "It becomes, 'Now what?'… and 'Yeah, but, this is what I need to do,' right?"

CASE STUDY: JOHN PAUL DEJORIA—FROM MOPPING UP TO CLEANING UP

Another incredible example, arguably even more extreme than Devon Harris, is the billionaire John Paul Dejoria. In 1980, when he co-founded the Paul Mitchell hair product company that established him, he was literally living in a 20-year-old automobile, having grown up in and out of foster care, served in the Navy, and worked a succession of menial jobs.

However, he and Paul Mitchell took out a $700 loan and got to work. He had some experience working in hair salons and being an entry-level employee at Redken Laboratories, so he had an inkling of what he was doing. The pair developed hair products and began selling them to local salons while expanding quickly. The gamble paid off, and after six years, the company was turning over $100 million. By 2022, it was valued at over $1 billion.[43]

Subsequently, Dejoria bought the rights to Patrón tequila from Mexico and began distributing it in the United States, initially to restaurants and friends to keep it exclusive (and therefore more desirable). That company is now also worth billions of dollars.[44]

All the odds were against Dejoria succeeding. He was from the wrong side of the tracks and had been hustling to survive since he was just nine years old. He'd been fired from jobs and had worked as a janitor, mopping up after everyone else. That could have been his position in life. He could have said, "Yeah, but this is where I'm from." It wasn't simple, and nothing was given to him. He had to work hard for it and take some big risks. But to reiterate Devon Harris, "You can't find new lands if you don't lose sight of the shoreline."

> **"Weigh the want for wins against the worries of woes."**
> **- Wolfe**ism

WHY DOES IT MATTER?

If you're going to start working through this Yeah, But, then it's time to start thinking about *why* where you're from restricts you from certain achievements. Is it because you grew up surrounded by people who fed you that idea, however subconsciously? Do your current peers tell you that? Is it that you've not witnessed what success looks like, and you've attached that idea to your roots? Is it because you feel attached to where you're from? Would you feel guilty about leaving your old life and your old friends and family behind, as if bettering yourself or following your dreams were some kind of betrayal? Do you feel that this is the life you're meant to have, and so you shouldn't argue with fate? (See *Yeah, But… What Will Others Say or Think?*)

Maybe you look at the statistics concerning people from your background, be it geographical, racial, sexual, ethnic, or whatever, and you see that they don't achieve what you want to accomplish. They don't have the same opportunities. They don't get to have that level of social mobility. If that's the case, then do the statistics say that 100% of people from your background don't get them? Or does it say 50% or 70%? Are those statistics even reliable? Does the small print say that their sample size was 1500, or only 15?

Either way, there *is* still opportunity, and it's there for you. Yes, *you*. See, in the context of this book, we're looking at what's possible, we are looking beyond the Yeah, But. People often overcome incredible odds to succeed. They don't all need to become billionaires to do so, but they might say, "Why can't you do it where I'm from? Why can't I be the first person from my family or neighborhood to go to college, start a successful business, build a new life elsewhere, or have a career as a corporate executive?"

IT'S WHERE YOU'RE AT

This has to be more than just words, though. As inspiring as words can be, you have to plant the seed in your mind, too. If you have the vision in your mind, then you can start acknowledging it. You can then start seeking out the people and the resources who can assist in elevating you to that level. That way, you see yourself differently. You shift your mindset. You stop believing the lie.

There are always ways to turn things around. There are rarely absolutes. Wherever you are on your journey, I bet you could find someone who feels the same way you do and is already further down a similar route to the one you want to take, even if they're only one step ahead.

At an even more basic level, what strengths have you discovered coming where you're from? What kind of resilience and work ethic were imparted to you? Positive traits like that are universally applicable. They're also a motivating factor for Devon Harris, who may have transcended his roots but has certainly never forgotten them. Back in 2006, he set up the Keep on Pushing Foundation, which came from his desire to help children growing up in his old neighborhood. Today, the foundation funds a breakfast club for pupils and provides other supplies, all in the hope that pupils will grow up with, "Yeah, but you *can* where I'm from" mentality.

And even if there aren't, what's keeping *you* from being the one to buck the perceived trend? If you went out there and achieved your dream, if you were in the other part of the percentages—the ones that *do* succeed—what would that mean for others who will be inspired by you taking action? What shift in other people's mindsets could that affect? This alone is obviously not a justification for wanting to achieve something because, above all else, you have to want to do it for yourself, or if you are like me, you do it because of your purpose; it has to resonate and align with you first and foremost. However, this is the kind of bonus that can add some extra motivation for you when you try turning this Yeah, But around.

Finally, on this topic, it's not just about dreaming. It's about action too. It's about acknowledging where you're from, but it's far more about where you're at and what you're doing about it.

BUT BUSTERS:

What values or lessons did you learn from your family or childhood environment that shape your work ethic and determination today?

_____
_____
_____
_____
_____
_____

What skills and attributes have you developed through overcoming challenges, and how do they prepare you for success in business?

_____
_____
_____
_____
_____
_____

Who in your life or circle has defied expectations and demonstrated that it's possible to achieve success, even when the statistics suggest otherwise?

_____
_____
_____
_____
_____

How can you leverage your uniqueness and story to set yourself apart from others?

_____
_____
_____
_____
_____

What's the first step you plan to take now that you've read this chapter?

_____
_____
_____

Congratulations! You've started busting this Yeah, But!

YEAH, BUT... I'M NOT QUALIFIED

12

A logical question to ask yourself at first is "Am I even able to do this?". After all, there are requirements for all types of roles, jobs, and careers. You might tell yourself that you don't have the right qualifications, that you haven't done your 10,000 hours of practice to be good enough, or that others are simply better than you.

And, of course, there will always be someone telling you that you can't do something because you don't have whatever it is that, in their mind, they think you need to bring an idea to life or get a project over the finish line. You don't have the "right" certificate, the "right" number of years of experience, or the "right" amount of insight, background, or exposure.

There's a different way of looking at it, though. Think about surgeons. You need qualifications and years of medical school to be a surgeon. But if you've ever required surgery, have you ever thought about whether your surgeon finished top, middle, or bottom of their class? They still perform the procedure regardless, right? So, we can quickly see that *qualifications* don't necessarily equal *quality*. They're absolutely necessary, and it's important that they exist, yet when you apply that thinking to your own situation, do you genuinely believe that a piece of paper or doing something for an arbitrary amount of time is what makes you qualified to start something?

FIGHTING THE FEAR OF BEING "FOUND OUT"

This is a Yeah, But that can manifest itself as the dreaded Impostor Syndrome, which is something that even the most outwardly successful people can suffer. In 2024, a study of American CEOs found that 71% had experienced Impostor Syndrome in their role at some point.[45]

But what exactly is Impostor Syndrome? It's the feeling that you might get "found out" somehow, and that other people will discover the truth about you—that you shouldn't have this job, be running this company, or earn this much money.

Let's think about that and start busting this Yeah, But right away. Let's think about how people who we'd consider public figures—CEOs of major companies, actors, athletes, etc. Tom Hanks, Serena Williams, people at or near the top of their game. They get Impostor Syndrome, just like you might. Underneath it all, despite their obvious talents and qualities, they feel unqualified to be doing the thing that has made their name.

Why should you be any different? If those who've succeeded have done so despite hearing the nagging little voice telling them (falsely) that they're not good enough, then why can't you succeed too? Thoughts are automatic, so we know that we might not be able to stop having Impostor Syndrome ones. The difference is that we can *choose* not to let them hold us back.

The key is knowing that you're supposed to be doing what you're doing. You may not be "qualified" in the sense that, okay, you might not be the absolute best in your given field. You might not be the most well-known. You may not even be the most insightful or organized. You might not even be presenting anything completely new. But is that enough to stop you from even trying?

This book is a great example. It may not be entirely new information. I may not be the most distinguished in my field.

However, I know that I'm *supposed* to be writing it. I know that the way I'm presenting this information, through my unique experiences and individual tone of voice, has the potential to affect you in a way that others writing on this subject won't. It doesn't matter that many of our foundational ideas may well be the same.

It's about being able to use your skills and talents to affect people's lives in a way that no one else can. Only you and you alone can present an idea or sell a product in a way that connects with them.

The world is packed with examples of people who could have let this Yeah, But hold them back, particularly when others told them they weren't qualified. Yet they succeeded anyway.

CASE STUDY: JOY MANGANO'S PERILOUS PATH TO SUCCESS

Joy Mangano came from a working-class background in Long Island, New York. She was a single mother of three children, trying to make ends meet by working as a waitress and an airline-reservation manager. One day, while cleaning up after her kids for the thousandth time, she had an idea that a self-wringing mop would make life so much easier for her.

Mangano had little experience in business, engineering, or inventing. She had few investors or connections either, and most of the people she did approach for help were skeptical of her idea.

She could have listened to those who were supposedly more experienced and more qualified, but Mangano was convinced that her idea could be a success. Even with the support of her father and some other backers, she still needed to take out loans and use what little savings she had as she began working out how to get her self-wringing mop made and on the market. She faced constant production challenges and had to try balancing her belief that she was supposed to be the one to bring this project to fruition against her responsibilities as a single working mother of three young children.

Eventually, though, in 1992, Mangano launched the Miracle Mop on the QVC shopping channel. Sales were initially slow, but Mangano was eventually allowed on-air to sell the mops herself. Again, this could have held her back—she'd never been on TV before, and she certainly wasn't a professional host. But then something happened. Mangano's passion and personality connected with viewers. The Miracle Mop eventually sold out, and Mangano embarked on a new career as an entrepreneur and inventor.[46]

This didn't mean her path was still clear. She would still face hurdles and legal challenges, but over 30 years later, no one can deny that she has become a highly successful woman with multiple innovative cleaning products to her name. She has even been the subject of a biopic called *Joy,* in which she was played by Jennifer Lawrence (who won a Golden Globe for her performance).

CASE STUDY: SUNEERA MADHANI AND PROOF THAT UNICORNS EXIST!

Suneera Madhani is a second-generation immigrant born in Chicago to Pakistani parents. While working for a credit card company in the early 2010s, she realized that there was a gap in the market for a subscription-based credit card payment processing platform. She pitched the idea to her company's management, and they literally laughed her out of the meeting room.

Frustrated, Madhani told her parents what had happened. They suggested she could launch the company herself, but she immediately replied with variations on the "Yeah, but I'm not qualified" theme: she had no experience in developing platforms, no industry connections, and no investors waiting in the wings.

Encouraged by her parents, however, she eventually gave herself six months to succeed. She raised $20,000 in capital from her savings and loans from friends and family to get herself afloat. Before the six months were up, her platform, then called Fattmerchant but now called Stax, had processed millions of dollars in credit card payments. Before long, the company had become a "unicorn startup," meaning it was valued at more than $1 billion.[47]

So you see that Madhani wasn't technically qualified to succeed with her idea. Not only that but those who were technically qualified laughed at her idea because they couldn't see the value. However, independent businesses were thrilled to have a payment processing platform that charged a flat fee rather than taking a per-transaction cut. They neither knew nor cared that Madhani's idea had been laughed at. Nor did it matter that she wasn't a professional developer. Her business model and her way of putting it across connected with them and made their lives easier. And importantly for Madhani, despite her initial Yeah, Buts, she had learned to trust her gut. She knew that her idea could work, and she went for it.

> *"The outcomes you demanded have not yet landed."*
>
> *- **Wolfe**ism*

"WHY" IS MORE IMPORTANT THAN "WHEN"

If you're waiting for the perfect moment, for the time when you're qualified to do something (I'm obviously not talking about brain surgery here), then you'll never get started. The perfect time is just like tomorrow. It never comes. If you don't do it, somebody else will. Elsewhere, we also discuss how somebody else is probably *already* out there doing it (see *Yeah, But... Somebody Already Did It*). But is that a reason for you not to try?

Even if you embark on something and make mistakes, then you still got your idea out there. At least you tried. And you will learn from those mistakes. If it stumbles, you'll fail forward. Remember, almost nothing is failure-proof. Even if you've got all the certificates and hours under your belt you could possibly get, there will always be an element of risk and of things not working out.

The important thing to keep in mind is to understand *why* you're doing what you're doing and what your role is. The women in the case studies above, plus countless other successful entrepreneurs, were, on paper, nowhere near the "best" or the "right" people for the job. That's why those who seemed better on paper were skeptical.

But Joy Mangano and Suneera Madhani didn't let this particular Yeah, But stop them. Yes, they had fears and setbacks and had to face rejection, but their "why" was stronger than all of that. They knew that they were the right people to bring their vision to life. They had just as much, if not more, desire for what they were doing than those at the top of that particular industry, and while that wasn't the only factor in their success, it was one of the motivating factors.

We don't only have to look at individuals, either. Some of the biggest household names on the planet go through this too. They have products that don't work, have to issue product recalls, and launch apps that need constant updates. They have all the means at their disposal to make things work—the budgets, the talent—but they still make mistakes. They're far more qualified than you or I, but they still fall short and have to make adjustments.

Does this mean that they're not good at what they do? Of course not. It's about being agile and about showing up—at least making it to market with your product or service. Take a chance, a step forward, take constructive feedback, and adjust your footing as you go.

Most companies in the United States are small businesses. Think locally about any of the independent companies that you use, the local restaurant or takeout that you visit so often they know your order by heart. Is their chef as qualified as, say, a Michelin-star chef? Contrast that with a famous chef whose food you tried and didn't like. Does that disqualify that very accomplished and certified chef? No. It's another opinion that shows fame, fortune, and certification don't magically make you perfect, likeable, or able to make everyone love what you provide.

So it's clear now, or it should be, that the ways in which we measure someone's qualification to perform a certain task or reach a certain level of achievement aren't always the best yardsticks. And even if they are, they don't preclude failures along the way. It doesn't matter if you're a novice or a pro. You don't win a game without making any moves, so own your move forward.

BUT BUSTERS:

If credentials were the sole criteria for success, then how would anything untried ever get started? What ideas and concepts of yours need refining to help you and the ideas grow?

_____

_____

_____

_____

_____

_____

When the world looks at new ideas, it doesn't always embrace them. What concept or practice did you not originally welcome but has now become an indispensable part of your work or personal life?

___

When you think about this Yeah, But, how much are you thinking, "It's just not possible", and how much are you thinking, "What if it could work?"

___

Traditional qualification requirements often reflect outdated traditions more than actual necessity. Maybe it's time to rewrite the rules. How might you apply your unique assets and experiences to your list of "qualifications"?

___

What's the first step you plan to take now that you've read this chapter?

_____
_____
_____

Congratulations! You've started busting this Yeah, But!

CLIENT CASE STUDY:
GABRIELLE THOMPSON– THE YEAH, BUTS OF AN INSPIRATIONAL YOUNG LEADER

Gabrielle is a truly remarkable woman. In 2015, at only 25 years old, she was appointed CEO of Free for Life International, a non-profit dedicated to combating human trafficking and helping its survivors. Yet despite her success and the vital importance of her work, she first came to me because of obstacles she was struggling to overcome alone. "I wanted to grow, be challenged, have someone be honest with me and call me forward to being a better leader," she explains. "I needed someone to push me to become a better leader and get over the things in my own way that created a harder path of leadership."

Once I began working with Gabrielle, we realized that the obstacles in her way were effectively three Yeah, Buts: "I'm afraid," "I'm too young," and "I'm not qualified." I did indeed challenge her to grow and empowered her with tools, such as BUMPT™ (see *Yeah, But... I Don't Have Time*), to help her move past these particular Yeah, Buts.

One of Gabrielle's Yeah, Buts–"Yeah, but I'm too young"–stemmed from her incredible career success at a young age. Becoming the CEO of an international non-profit organization in your mid-twenties is a fantastic achievement however you look at it. It should also go without saying that Gabrielle was picked for the job for a reason. By her mid-teens, her fascination with the lives of women and girls in other countries had hardened into a resolve to dedicate her life to working with them, especially when they were denied the basic freedoms she took for granted growing up in the United States. "These are my sisters. I want to serve them," was her mantra.

To start working toward her goal, Gabrielle majored in Global Studies and then completed a Master's in International Affairs at Middle Tennessee State University (MTSU). Just a year after graduation, she went for an interview at Nashville-based Free for Life International and was appointed CEO almost immediately. "[Free for Life founder Colette Wise] offered me the job without even reading my resumé," Gabrielle later recalled in an interview. This annoyed her a little, as she felt it didn't fully respect all the hard work she'd put into getting herself shortlisted in the first place.

Her appointment also brought with it a lot of baggage and assumptions—people were projecting their Yeah, Buts about age onto her. "Right off the bat, I was too young within what people would perceive as how old you can become a leader," she told me when I interviewed her for *The Yeah, But Podcast*. "It was a challenge because stepping into a place of leadership, but not feeling like there was appropriate respect because of my youth, made me really question myself at the time: 'The world is telling me I'm too young to be a leader. Can I do this?'"

But she could do it. In fact, she was soon doing things that most leaders twice her age would shy away from. Within months of starting, she was in India, witnessing first-hand the 30-block brothel district that her organization worked to free women from. She even stayed in the safe house that sheltered trafficking survivors as young as six years old. Characteristically, her biggest Yeah, But in terms of fear was not for her physical safety but that she wouldn't be able to do her role justice.

Ultimately, however, she led Free for Life for eight years. What she witnessed in the red-light districts, brothels, safe houses, and orphanages of the world broke her heart, but out of that heartbreak, positive action was forged. Under her leadership, Free for Life expanded its international reach and developed new programs to help the female victims of human trafficking. "I feel like I've grown a lot," Gabrielle says, looking back. "I understand that age is not a barrier to leadership; it's more about how you handle the opportunity of leadership. It's more about the wisdom, experience, and what [an organization is] willing to give their level of leadership, but I didn't realize that at the time."

Reflecting on her time as a young CEO leading vital, sensitive work, Gabrielle told me that what could have helped her navigate her early Yeah, Buts was being more intentional. "How can I create a care plan? How can I make sure I'm being intentional about the way I'm grieving and what comes out of it? How am I going to turn this into action?" she explained. "It happened naturally, but I wish I'd been more intentional about preparing to ask myself those questions."

In 2022, Gabrielle moved on to become CEO of another global non-profit organization, IDEAS (International Development and Educational Associates). Although still young by most boardroom standards, she was now equipped with almost a decade of experience leading international non-profits. But that didn't mean that all her Yeah, Buts had been vanquished.

One of the first things she wanted to do was dramatically revamp the almost-30-year-old organization—"basically tearing the house down to the studs." The fear-based Yeah, Buts were still there, however. "There were significant implications for the organization and our personnel across the world," she told me. "If I failed, it would significantly influence the lives of so many families. That was very scary. It made me question, "If I fail, how will that shift my own identity of what I think I'm capable of?"

It was around this time that Gabrielle came to me for executive coaching. She was seeking not only advice but also pushback—people who weren't afraid to suggest if she was headed in the wrong direction and to challenge her to keep raising her game. "You called me forward to being the authentic version of myself," she told me of our coaching sessions. "You helped me establish better boundaries, shifted my leadership with my team to an empowerment model, and helped me to transform how I use my time."

Of course, Gabrielle still faces fear-based Yeah, Buts today, particularly now that IDEAS is implementing her proposed radical revamp, but her rationale for working past them rings with advice found elsewhere in this book, whatever your goal is: "There are really only two options: I can be afraid of failure and keep things the same, or I can move forward into knowing that I may fail, but at least I tried, at least I wanted to stretch to achieve something greater than what I thought possible."

YEAH, BUT... I DON'T FEEL SUCCESSFUL 13

The first question to ask yourself if not feeling successful is holding you back is, "Okay... what does success feel like?", because straight off the bat, you're implying that success is a *feeling*. And you're implying that you know what it feels like because you're feeling the opposite, right?

When working through these kinds of Yeah, Buts—those you tell yourself—it's essential to look inside and truly come to grips with what they mean. That way, you can cut through all the meaningless noise and hone in on defining who you are and what you want to achieve. Reaching goals requires clarity. You have to have a specific target that you want to reach—you need to know what you want and be able to articulate it.

Too often, we view success relatively: we think we're not as successful as our parents, our friends, our peers, or our coworkers. Sometimes, we even weigh our perceived lack of success against people we've never met. How ridiculous is that?! Such comparison games are a trap. They hinder us because we can end up adjusting our goals to match those of others.

It can work the other way, too. You might find that you're letting others define what success looks like for you. Again, this could be anyone in your life. You might buy into the stereotypical career and material dreams that you *think* you should have because it'll make you happy (and because you think it's what everyone else wants?). You might feel that your social or cultural background means that you must hit certain targets, regardless of whether you want to or whether they're in your best interests.

I heard this quote, which has been attributed to different people over the years: "We spend money we don't have on things we don't need to impress people we don't even like." It's uncomfortably true, and it also highlights how often we do things for the benefit of others rather than ourselves. See, there's a big difference between being of meaningful service to others and working against our own interests while making ourselves unhappy in the process.

If we *do* want to look at success relatively, then instead of looking up, why don't we look down or across? You might be thinking, "But I *am* doing this for myself, Marc. I truly want to be successful!" Okay, well, do you have running water? Then you're already more prosperous than almost 30% of people in the world today. Even if you only have the basics, you're living in the kind of luxury that many people in the world only dream of having. Does that provide some perspective? Can you see that success is a metric best linked to gratitude? It can come down to a choice between playing the comparison game or focusing on your gratitude.

As we discuss in other chapters, you're you, and you're unique. Let's prove it: research has shown that no two people have the same ear shape. You can be identified by just the shape of your ears with around 99% accuracy. So it follows that you will naturally have different needs and goals from others, even if only by the smallest fraction. Projecting your desires onto others or letting them project theirs onto you isn't going to have a healthy outcome. You usually end up veering off your own course and possibly living to regret it. You have to know what you want for yourself and then work out the most suitable way for you to go and get it. What if you could attain your goals because you're *not* the people you compare yourself to? What if your individualistic skills could help you achieve the goals that work best for you?

Look, this isn't a psychology book. This is a practical guide to getting out of your own way and growing an understanding of what you're on this planet to achieve. You can't do that if you spend too much of your time measuring yourself against others or letting other people define your success on their terms.

> *"Prioritize what you want to emphasize."*
> **- Wolfe**ism

CASE STUDY: ANDRE AGASSI, THE TENNIS LEGEND WHO HATED TENNIS

The world of fame is littered with stories of people who achieved success beyond even their own wildest dreams, only to find themselves unfulfilled. Examples can be found in sports, film and television, music, politics, and big business. The backstory is almost always a variation on the same theme: a talented kid who is either pushed extremely hard by their parents (who are often living vicariously through their child) or who pushes themselves in a subconscious bid to win the love and validation they feel they never had.

Either way, whatever they achieve, they remain fundamentally unhappy and rarely *feel* successful and fulfilled. They might try to fill the void with even greater levels of success, material possessions, wild partying, alcohol, or drugs, but that obviously never works, and it rarely ends well.

There have been many examples of this tragic story over the years, from Shirley Temple to Britney Spears. Michael Jackson is perhaps the most extreme example, but one example we can take something positive from is that of legendary tennis player Andre Agassi.

From a very young age, Agassi was pushed by his ambitious father, a former Olympic boxer. He wanted him to become a major tennis star and had a "win-at-all-costs" mentality. His insistence on endless practice and competing in junior tournaments robbed the young Andre of a more "normal" childhood. He was forced to quit playing other sports he enjoyed, such as soccer, in order to adhere to his father's harsh "5,000 balls a day" training regime.[48]

Agassi turned pro at 16 and went on to become one of the most famous and successful tennis players of all time, winning eight Grand Slam titles and an Olympic gold medal between 1992 and 2003. He was ranked the world's number-one player in 1999, and his career winnings totaled more than $30 million. At one point, he married Hollywood actress Brooke Shields.[49] On the face of it, he had everything.

Yet, Agassi hated tennis! He actually *hated* it. In his autobiography, *Open*, he would call it the "loneliest" sport in the world, saying, "Where else do you see people talk to themselves that much, right? And answer themselves?"[50]

It's little surprise, then, that no matter how many trophies, accolades, or millions he got, Agassi never felt fulfilled—never felt successful—and started seeking ways to escape. At the height of his fame, he even began taking crystal meth. Of course, this led to a failed drug test. Around the same time, his marriage to Brooke Shields began to fall apart. He started losing more matches, and his place in the world rankings plummeted. He'd hit rock bottom.[51]

However, once he'd hit the lowest point, Agassi finally began to address how he'd ended up so successful and so deeply unhappy at the same time. Through therapy, he began to address his childhood issues and move away from his father's definition of success. He eventually arrived at a place where he could enjoy tennis a little more. Also, he began giving back through philanthropy, setting up charities to help children reach their athletic potential, and schools for "at-risk" children.[52]

This helped Agassi embark on a new phase of his career, one that was arguably more successful than the first. He regained his place at the top of the world tennis rankings and would play at the highest level for another seven years before retiring.

In short, Andre Agassi had it all. But it wasn't the kind of all that he wanted, and he ended up on seriously destructive drugs as a result. At least part of the reason why was that success had been defined for him by someone else. Because of this, it didn't matter how successful he got, it wasn't the kind of success that was aligned with who he was, so it didn't fulfill him. Only when he realized this and started working out what he truly wanted could he begin to come to terms with his success and get some value from it.

MOVE THROUGH IT

Your story doesn't need to be as wildly dramatic as Andre Agassi's so you can experience something similar. It doesn't need to involve world titles, Hollywood marriages, or Schedule II drugs. You might have ended up in a corporate career that you don't enjoy, but you embarked on it because that's what was "expected" of you. Ultimately, if it doesn't fulfill you, then it doesn't matter how high you climb; you will never feel successful.

I learned long ago that the purely conditionally focused approach—"If I have x, then I'll be happy"—doesn't work. Never has, never will. We see this with children. They can nag their parents into buying this or that toy from the store, only to lose interest in it within minutes when they finally get their way. We can end up doing the same thing as adults, throwing money at houses, cars, certain clothing brands, and the latest technology. It's particularly exhausting and frankly irrational if you're doing it to impress others, whether it's your friends, family, or social media followers.

Even if you think you're doing it for a reason, it might not always be the right reason, as the case of Andre Agassi and countless others shows. Not all of them had a happy ending, either. There are people who spend their lives chasing the success they thought would make them happy, only to die penniless and bitter without ever having gotten there. In doing so, they didn't realize they were chasing the wind. They were so focused on theoretical happiness in the future that they forgot to take stock of the successes they were achieving in the present. They might have felt more content if they'd paused and reflected on how far they'd come.

Is that the kind of life you want? What kind of legacy do *you* want to leave behind?

See, there's a big difference in approach here, and it can often determine whether you feel successful or not. You can define a goal and work toward it step-by-step, enjoying the journey as you go and celebrating your milestones along the way. Or you can define a goal and become mindlessly fixated on it, grimly clawing your way toward it, convinced that nothing else matters and that you won't be happy until you get there. Even if the goal in both scenarios aligns with your values, which process do you think will be more fulfilling? Which do you think will make you feel more successful?

USE THE RIGHT METAPHOR

There are dozens of metaphors I could use here. I could say it's like this or that, but there's a danger with metaphors that people don't always realize. They can come with a lot of baggage and restrictions because you must alter the message you want to convey to fit the metaphor.

For example, let's say you're working on a project, and you compare it to a marathon runner in a race. Okay, well, yes, you and the metaphorical runner are both working to reach a goal, to get from A to B in a good time without burning out.

So far, so good. But what if your project hits a roadblock and needs to take a different route? What if you need to adjust the end goal a little? Well, a marathon runner can't do that. Their course has been laid out in advance. They don't get to choose where the finish line is. What if you realize you need to take a little time away? Or retrace your steps a little? Again, a marathon runner doesn't do that. They don't pull up a chair halfway through to rest their legs, and they certainly don't go back and run a certain mile over again because they feel they could have run it better!

The metaphor doesn't fit. It's no big deal, but by using such a seemingly fitting metaphor, are you subconsciously tying yourself to *the* idea that you *are* a marathon runner who must take a set route to reach an unmovable finish line? Don't let strong-sounding metaphors hold you back or hem you in.

BUT BUSTERS

How does success resonate with you on a personal level?

_____

_____

_____

_____

_____

When defining success for yourself, do you find alignment with your core values?

Do you tend to overlook positive feedback while dwelling on the negative? How might you shift this perspective?

How has measuring your progress against others affected your self-confidence?

With what recent achievements or areas of personal development do you find cause for celebration?

_____
_____
_____
_____
_____
_____

What's the first step you plan to take now that you've read this chapter?

_____
_____
_____

Congratulations! You've started busting this Yeah, But!

YEAH, BUT... WHAT WILL OTHERS SAY OR THINK? 14

Oh, they're already saying and thinking things, my friend. One sure thing about humans is that we all have opinions. Historically, we've not always shared them, but the advent of social media has got millions of people oversharing their thoughts on everything from sports to politics to food to what other people choose to name their children. Whether they're informed or not is irrelevant.

There's nothing you can do about that. People are invariably going to have opinions, both said and unsaid, about you and what you're doing. You'll likely always wonder what people think about you or say when you're not there, but it only becomes an issue if you let it. Remember, this isn't about other people. It has more to do with you, what you're doing, and why you're doing it.

Here's the thing: sometimes people can become so affected by what others are doing that they end up having stronger opinions on your life and goals than anything in their own lives. Many times, this is based on their insecurity. They attempt to project their shortcomings and their limiting beliefs onto you and what you're doing. Whichever way they dress it up, it boils down to them saying, "If I can't do it, then you shouldn't be able to either." It may stem from jealousy, low self-esteem, or even their current or past situation. Whatever it is, the bottom line is that it produces unhelpful insights. What gives anyone the right to tell you that you can't or shouldn't be able to do something simply because *they* can't?

CONSTRUCTIVE OR DESTRUCTIVE?

It's important to remember this when it comes to advice and feedback. There's a big difference between constructive criticism—which is thought out, insightful, perceptive, and offers ways forward—and destructive criticism, which only seeks to tear you down with no supporting evidence or data. The latter is just someone dumping all their own Yeah, Buts onto you. This would be a good time to hand them a copy of this book.

What makes this a Yeah, But for you, and how do you want to move past it? Is your biggest concern really that others might have negative things to say about what you're doing? Or do you have more important reasons for doing it? Is the purpose behind it or your end goal more significant than getting caught up in your estimation of what other people's perceptions might be?

Whether you do it or not, people are going to be affected either way. So there's a choice to make at that juncture. Do you want to affect people's lives positively by taking action or impact them negatively by standing still? Either way, people are going to have a perception and opinion of you, and it's ultimately up to you how much of a role you want to have in shaping that perception through your actions or inaction.

Ask yourself how others would see you if you missed an opportunity and didn't go through with something you said you wanted to do. Then, ask yourself how others would see you if you made a move and took action toward that thing. If you acted positively or offered positive words that others needed to hear.

Picture this: you're leading a team tasked with launching a new product. There's a risk involved, and you're shouldering the bulk of responsibility. There are essentially two ways forward: play it safe and avoid potential criticism and pushback, or step up, make bolder moves, risk a few raised eyebrows, but ultimately drive the project forward.

If you're going to be talked about, how would you rather it be? As someone who toed the line, afraid to make ripples, or someone who, regardless of the result, put themselves out there and tried to take it up a level?

When you keep your purpose, your "why," paramount in your mind, then you can begin aligning yourself with the reality of what is actually happening and what's genuinely at stake rather than getting lost in a fog of what other people may or may not think. Let's be real here: will most of the people whose opinions you're concerned about be affected by whatever happens? If not, why does their opinion matter so much?

Of course, adopting this perspective is often easier said than done. Too many of us have been conditioned for most of our lives to care what other people think. This isn't without its value because we have to be mindful of our responsibilities as part of a wider community and society. However, there comes a time when being mindful of what others think (or might think) begins holding us back unnecessarily. Yes, there are times when it's right to consider other's thoughts and feelings and to take their advice. But there are equally times when you've got to persevere. Being able to tell the difference between the two is part of becoming an effective leader and a more confident human being.

> *"Just because you perceive it doesn't mean you should believe it."*
>
> — **Wolfe**ism

CASE STUDY: JERRIE MOCK—MAKING A MOCKERY OF YEAH, BUTS

Jerrie Mock is a great example of what can be achieved when we follow our purpose and don't let outside voices discourage us. The pioneering aviator defied societal norms and soared into history as the first woman to fly solo around the world in 1964. Her remarkable journey, undertaken in a single-engine Cessna 180 named *The Spirit of Columbus,* spanned 22,860 miles and 21 stopovers in 29 days.[53]

Born Geraldine Fredritz in 1925, Mock grew up during the dark days of the Great Depression. Despite, or perhaps because of this, her fascination with aviation started at a young age. She defied the gender stereotypes of the time and pursued flying, becoming the only woman in her aviation engineering class at Ohio State University. She was looked down on by most of her male classmates, yet that changed when she went on to become the only class member to get a perfect score on a high-level chemistry exam.

Mock dropped out of college in 1945 to marry and become a housewife. She and her husband had three kids, but the domestic routine of the time and the stereotypical housewife duties she was expected to perform left her unfulfilled.[54] She felt she had something more to achieve for herself, for women, and for her beloved aviation. So, when her kids were at school, she began taking flying lessons. Soon, she and her husband were qualified pilots and they'd purchased a plane.

Yet for Mock, it still wasn't enough. One evening at dinner, as she was railing against the lack of excitement in her life, her husband challenged her to fly around the world in their plane. She accepted the challenge and began making it a reality. She took out loans and got her plane modified so that it was up for the trip.

Mock's historic flight was not without challenges, though. As well as having to face limited flying experience and technological constraints, she also found herself in a media-created "race" against a more experienced, also-female pilot who was planning to undertake the same round-the-world trip. To make things worse, when she set off on the first leg of her trip, she overheard an air traffic controller say to his co-worker, "I guess that's the last we'll hear from her."

Mock could have let such opinions ground her, but she used them as fuel. She embarked on her journey with determination and meticulous planning. Despite setbacks and the looming competition from the other pilot, she persevered, pushing herself beyond her limits to achieve her goal.

Throughout her journey, Mock encountered obstacles ranging from technical difficulties to unexpected landings at military bases. Yet she remained calm under pressure, showcasing her remarkable skill and resilience. Ultimately, her journey took her across continents, allowing her to fulfill her childhood dreams of riding camels and elephants and seeing the pyramids.

Her triumphant return to Ohio just under a month after leaving was met with accolades and recognition. She had cemented her legacy as a trailblazer in aviation history. Life wasn't always so rosy for her afterward—she suffered financial challenges and other setbacks—but she had pursued her goal to its end, always remembering her purpose. She also won the "race" against the other pilot.

One of many great things about Mock's story is that it provides an ongoing legacy, inspiring women and other hopeful young aviators all these years later. One example is professional Afghani pilot Shaesta Waiz, who became the youngest woman to circumnavigate the globe in 2017.[55] The main goals of her flight were to promote science, technology, engineering, and math (STEM) education for women and girls globally and to inspire them to pursue careers in aviation and other STEM fields.

WHAT MATTERS MORE?

Jerrie Mock's story is an excellent example of how to bust through this Yeah, But. It shows the level of achievement that can be attained when you don't let what others think or say hold you back. It proves that you can make a difference in your own life and those of others, including those you've never met and never will meet.

As the story also shows, it's not always easy. It can involve taking risks and learning new skills. But it can be accomplished, and the results can cause positive ripples that last beyond your lifetime.

Not being a prisoner of other people's opinions is as much a question of acceptance as it is changing your perspective. We saw at the beginning of this chapter that people are often going to make assumptions and have opinions. Sometimes, they'll be valid. Sometimes, they'll be so far off-base that you'll be astonished. Occasionally, they'll be verbalized. Other times, they won't.

And why shouldn't other people have opinions anyway? I bet you do it as well, sometimes without even realizing it. It's what many of us do. The key is to know your priorities. What, to you, are the three most important outcomes of your project or your idea? Do others' opinions mean so much that it negates what you wanted to accomplish in the first place?

There's another way of looking at this, too. Do you have the right to define other people's perceptions of you and your work? Now that's a deep one because, on one level, of course you do. We all want those we respect to think the best of us. Who would want to be disliked by their peers? But at the same time, you can't force people to like or agree with you. You can't tell them what to think about you. You can try, but it won't work in the long run.

What you can do and what you *do* have the right to do is help shape people's perceptions of you. And that involves taking action to move ideas from where they are to what they can be. It involves pushing this Yeah, But aside and taking chances. Those who are meant to hear what you've got to say will hear it and understand it. Those who don't get it aren't your audience.

OPINIONS < GAINS

You should now be able to see why and how you need to turn this Yeah, But around. Other people have opinions. What's new? Do those opinions contain any constructive advice or feedback? If so, great. If not, so what? As long as you know how to discern which is which, then what does it truly matter if others have a negative opinion of you and what you're doing, especially when it's often a projection of their own insecurities?

What's your purpose for doing or wanting to do what you're doing? That's the thing you've got to keep right there in the front of your mind. Do the potential benefits of accomplishing it outweigh the fear of others' opinions? Just as crucially, will *not* doing it affect how people see you for the better?

The long and short of this Yeah, But is that you can't make what fuels it go away. You can't stop people from thinking thoughts and having opinions–good, bad, or otherwise. That's the makings of dystopian fiction. The best you can do is help to perhaps shape those opinions by looking at this Yeah, But within the wider context of what you and others stand to gain if you don't let it hold you back.

BUT BUSTERS

If you're going to be known for something, would you rather be known as someone who tried and failed or as someone who never tried?

_____
_____
_____
_____
_____
_____

How can you acknowledge that perceptions already exist, whether we act or stay silent?

_____
_____
_____
_____
_____
_____

What would it look like if you focused on internal motivations over external perceptions?

_____
_____
_____
_____
_____
_____

What next steps will you take to gradually reshape outdated perceptions of yourself and your skills?

_____
_____
_____
_____
_____

What's the first step you plan to take now that you've read this chapter?

_____
_____
_____

Congratulations! You've started busting this Yeah, But!

YEAH, BUT... WHAT IF I FAIL? 15

All too often, when we become afraid of failure, it's not because others have taught us to be afraid. It's because we've spent so long needlessly tormenting ourselves with the prospect of it. However, our fear of failure is often a projection of how we think others might view us if we fail. There's a lot of perceived embarrassment and shame involved with failure because it's a win-or-lose situation. If you're not a success, you're a failure. And who wants to be a failure, right?

At best, fear of failure can hinder our progress because we have to keep using valuable energy to fight it. At worst, it can paralyze us, so we never get started.

The emotions that failure stirs within us can be overwhelming. When a dream doesn't come true, we can find ourselves going through a kind of grief cycle, dealing with anger, despair, and sadness. It can make us not want to try again for fear of experiencing those emotions again. But there is hope. There is a way to reframe failure. Let's say that failing is when you don't complete 100% of what you set out to do. You set out to do a 10-mile run but only go eight miles before you have to give up because you're exhausted. Did you fail? Or did you run eight more miles than you would have done had you stayed sitting on your sofa?

Let's take this metaphor and look into it a little deeper. If you're moving toward anything—a goal, an outcome, a process—then the first stage is to address your Yeah, Buts and take positive, intentional steps, however small. Once you've done that, you've already got a measure of success right there. You've achieved more than you would have done by standing still.

I get it; there are times when you *feel* like you're in an all-or-nothing situation, when things are either done or not done, with no in-between. But even then, is that a definite reality, or can it be reframed as an iterative process? Can you think of each step as giving you a perspective and experience that you didn't have before?

Almost instantly, we have a fresh angle on "failure." The journey from where you are now to your desired endpoint is a process with multiple steps, each representing a milestone.

STOP SCARING YOURSELF

We humans can be very good at scaring ourselves, especially when our minds get preoccupied with what *might* happen in the future. This can mean anything from being freaked out by the strange noises our houses make at night to convincing ourselves that not only is our project doomed to failure but that others will also judge us, look down on us, and maybe even laugh at us.

Here is arguably the core of this Yeah, But: a fear of the *consequences* of failure. They might be material—you might lose money—or they might be social—the people around you will think less of you (see *Yeah, But… What Will Others Say or Think?*). Either way, when you begin to look a little more closely at your fear of failure, you can see that it's often based on a fear of what *could* happen, not what will definitely happen.

Sometimes, yes, you may have "failed" at something before. You may even have tried to do what you want to do now once before and not succeeded. But that's life; that's part of being human. As a baby, could you immediately walk or talk? No. It all took time to learn. But you kept trying by instinct, practicing and refining as you went.

Of course, as we grow we learn not to do certain things, like put our hands on something that will burn or scald. But that useful, purposeful fear, the one that keeps us safe, can also spread and hold us back from achieving something that will help us to thrive. It can keep us *too* safe. But nothing in life is wholly risk-free. You might get a paper cut reading this book, but is that reason enough not to read it?! (See *Yeah, But... It's Not Safe*)

Ultimately, whatever its root, this Yeah, But is based on self-preservation, not self-improvement. If you don't take that first step, if you stay right where you are, then you're good. But are you ever going to be great?

> **"Not looking for your flaw. Let's look for the fix."**
> — **Wolfe**ism

CASE STUDY: IF AT FIRST YOU DON'T SUCCEED, TRY AGAIN (5,127 TIMES IN THE CASE OF SIR JAMES DYSON)

A great example of resilience in the face of perceived failure is British inventor and entrepreneur Sir James Dyson, long renowned for his revolutionary contributions to household appliances.

When Sir James embarked on the creation of his first Dual Cyclone vacuum cleaner (one that did away with the traditional bag), little did he know that it would take a staggering 5,126 attempts before he achieved even a functional prototype.[56] Yet each setback, each failed iteration, served as a stepping stone toward his ultimate triumph. It was a journey, even if it did have more steps than he anticipated.

The genesis of Sir James' bagless vacuum cleaner was not without its challenges. Initially met with skepticism and rejection by British retailers, he faced an uphill battle to bring his innovation to market. Eventually, it was Japan that gave him the breakthrough that he needed. The success of his early models in their market paved the way for him to establish a research center in England where he could continue experimenting with different ideas. As he stated, "Life is a mountain of solvable problems."[57]

It's important to be aware that not all of Sir James' products worked. One, the CR01 washing machine, had to be discontinued because it cost too much to produce.[58] It was a very public "failure," not just a sketch that had been rejected. But Sir James is known for viewing failure not as a mark of defeat but as a badge of honor. It proves that he dares to take risks and push boundaries, and that takes courage.

Now we know that even the most successful people continue to take risks and embrace failure as part of a process. Just as importantly, we know that success doesn't solve all our problems or make us perfect. Not everything we do will turn to gold, however successful we become.

CASE STUDY: STEPHEN KING AND OVERCOMING THE HORROR OF FAILURE

Another area in which it's notoriously tough to succeed is literature. Almost every author has to prepare themselves for rejection and total indifference if they want their work published. If authors couldn't handle those things, then very few books would ever see the light of day.

Stephen King is one famous example of an author who had to fail before he flew. By his mid-twenties, he'd had a few short stories published in magazines, but success as an author of horror novels had eluded him. He'd tried writing them, but he'd always given up and scrapped them.

In 1973, he was halfway through yet another novel, *Carrie,* and was about to give up yet again. However, his wife encouraged him to keep going and finish it. He took her advice and completed the novel, only for it to then be rejected dozens of times by various agents. Then, finally, an agent took a chance on it, and within two years, it had sold over one million copies and was adapted into a feature film.[59]

Today, King is regarded as one of, if not *the* greatest horror writers of all time. His books have sold hundreds of millions of copies worldwide. But he had to endure failure—falling short of his end goal—first. He had to practice not giving up and moving forward through the process.

There are other books, multimillion-selling classics, that were also rejected an absurd number of times. *Chicken Soup for the Soul,* the world-renowned self-help book, was turned down by 144 publishers before being accepted! As one of its co-authors, Jack Canfield said, "If we'd given up after 100 publishers, I likely would not be where I am now."[60]

Multiple publishers also turned their noses up at books such as Stephen Covey's *Seven Habits of Highly Successful People* and Napoleon Hill's *Think and Grow Rich,* arguably two of the most essential books for any budding entrepreneur.

As well as remembering that achieving one's ultimate goal is often a step-by-step process with failure embedded along the way, we can also see that those in positions of relative power to us—those more "qualified"—aren't always right in their judgments. They fail too. No one is infallible. It doesn't matter if you're at the very top, right at the bottom, or somewhere in the middle.

THE BEST WAY TO DO IT IS BY LIVING THROUGH IT

A marathon is 26.2 miles long. To run one with no training whatsoever would be crazy, if not impossible. Those who train for marathons or any kind of endurance event build themselves up to being able to run that far, one milestone at a time, starting with much shorter runs, then trying to go a little further every time, tweaking and adjusting the process as necessary. Each time you successfully run a little further or a little faster, it's a tangible achievement and one step closer to the ultimate goal of running a full marathon.

In business, a process called Agile uses a similar methodology. It was originally used in software development but has also been adopted in other fields. It involves time-boxed periods, known as "sprints," which are usually between one and four weeks long. During each sprint, a team will plan, execute, review, and adapt. The aim is to have something functional to present to stakeholders that could theoretically be released to the public. The team will then use stakeholder feedback to embark on another sprint, further advancing and refining the product or the idea. This iterative process repeats until the project is complete.

Both examples show us that not reaching an end goal in one go doesn't equal failure. Far from it. They show us how we can break achieving our goals down into a process, into a series of opportunities for development and improvement. You start working toward your goal by getting your hands dirty and pushing and stretching yourself in directions you perhaps never thought possible before you started.

FAILING FORWARD

Hopefully, by now, you will appreciate how much overcoming this Yeah, But depends on shifting your perspective on what failure means. When you're worried that it *might* happen, then ask yourself, "What's the worst that could happen?" and be realistic about the possibilities. When it *does* happen, then it's not a negative reflection of your abilities, and it doesn't mean that there's anything wrong with you. Failure, in that sense, is always an opportunity to learn and grow.

I value the term "fail forward." You'll find it used elsewhere in this book. It means that every time we fall short of our desired goal, we're still nearer to it for having tried than if we'd done nothing. There are mistakes we can learn from and changes we can make as a result. Sure, we've "failed," but we've moved forward as an outcome. The distance between us and our endpoint is now nearer.

When we adopt and apply this viewpoint in our day-to-day lives, we adopt a "growth mindset." We're flipping the script and seeing the light of opportunity rather than the shadow of failure. We bring ourselves closer to that innate ability to experiment, learn, adapt, and evolve that helped us as babies when we learned to walk and talk.

Even if we fail at something multiple times, then as long as we don't keep repeating the same process without learning from our mistakes, we develop resilience too. We harden against the knocks and don't let them stop us from getting closer to our goals.

FEEDBACK

A major part of this is being open to forward-focused feedback. This can be a tough one for many people because it can involve others criticizing them, their work, and their ideas. But it's necessary to ask for that kind of feedback, even though it can feel uncomfortable.

It's part of the iterative process. It's a learning curve. You learn from your mistakes, but you can also learn from people who've already done what you want to do. Remember, there is nothing new under the sun. We're all reinventing the wheel to some extent. So, ask people who've already done it. Okay, their advice won't guarantee your success, but what's the worst that could happen? You get an extra perspective.

MEASURE GAINS, NOT LOSSES

Sometimes, failure is a fact of life. If we don't learn to accept it and move on from it in a healthy way, then we can come to view it as inevitable in everything we do. When that happens, we risk growing bitter, disillusioned, and unwilling to try.

Yes, occasionally, you may try your best and it may still not work out. But at every step of whatever it is you're working to accomplish, it's important to reflect and ask yourself what you've gained. It could be something tangible or just the experience of overcoming your fears and giving it your best shot.

Your failures punctuate your accomplishments. Don't focus on the period mark and ignore the sentence it goes with. Which has more value? Think back to the last time you set out to achieve something. Mine it for the value it added to your life and the lessons you took from it.

BUT BUSTERS:

Which fears or beliefs about failure are holding you back from pursuing your purpose?

_____
_____
_____
_____
_____
_____

How can you reframe your mindset around failure to view it as a natural part of the learning process?

_____
_____
_____
_____
_____

What small steps can you take to overcome your fear of failure and take action towards your goals?

_____
_____
_____
_____
_____

How can you cultivate a sense of determination and positivity in the face of setbacks?

_____
_____
_____
_____
_____

What's the first step you plan to take now that you've read this chapter?

_____
_____
_____

Congratulations! You've started busting this Yeah, But!

YEAH, BUT... NOW WHAT? 16

We're taught that every book has to have a conclusion. Fiction or nonfiction, all the threads need tying together to make a comprehensive and satisfying conclusion. Yet the truth is that, in books like this, most readers don't care about the conclusion because it brings nothing new to the table. All it does is restate everything the author just spent hundreds of pages explaining in great detail. There's no sense of excitement like there is when you first start a book and you feel yourself on the threshold of a new world, one that might change your life. So, we could say, "Yeah, but... why bother?" Why have a conclusion at all? Why not end the book after the last chapter? After all, I've said everything I came here to say.

But there is a conclusion here because I want you to take a moment to reflect on the Yeah, Buts that most resonated with you as you were reading this book. I'm willing to bet there were three or four that got to you, that pushed your buttons, because you know they're holding you back. Yet those Yeah, Buts—your Yeah, Buts—don't have to be a restraint. If you own them and resolve to work through them, they can be an invitation to embark on a new journey or revisit dreams you abandoned a long time ago. It can even be an invitation to shift your perspective by a single degree, and that small change can make all the difference.

Maybe you reach a place of acceptance—you live with your Yeah, Buts and work around them as best you can—or perhaps this is the moment you realize that you're ready to bust them for good.

Either way, having read this book and answered the But Busters at the end of each chapter, you're now in a better position to look at them objectively and decide whether what is holding you back stems from fear, an irrational belief, the desire for an unrealistic level of control, or maybe something you're still working to uncover. We can face our fears and rewire our beliefs, but we can't control every outcome.

The reality is that there's rarely a perfect moment for anything. Everything in life brings about some level of risk, and there will always be things that we can't predict or plan for. The wisest course of action, therefore, is to hold space for uncertainty. And, yes, that includes the potential for failure. Just as nothing is risk-proof, nothing is fail-proof either.

I'm not being cynical or trying to rain on your parade here; I'm simply saying don't let fear, risk, or uncertainty become such a huge Yeah, But that you never even start out toward your goal. Once you've done all you can to practically mitigate the chance of error or failure, then move forward knowing that none of us are perfect, that you will make mistakes, and that, above all else, the most important thing is to at least try.

The key word there is start. Whether your Yeah, But is one you've told yourself, one that others have told you, or a mixture of both, the way through it is to take action—however small that step might feel on the complex, multi-layered journey of your life. If you start out and things don't work out, then you're still further along the path, and you've still learned some valuable lessons for having taken action.

Some people call this "failing forward." I call it But Busting.

You might have noticed that I didn't share much about myself in this book, and I could offer up elaborate excuses why, but I'll be as honest with you here as I have been throughout: my Yeah, But is, "It's not about me." My coach and peers, who read early drafts of the book, advised me to include more of my story, but I still decided against it. This book is not my story; it's not an egotistical excuse to parade my achievements. It's not even so much about the people in the case studies, although their experiences are, of course, highly valuable. Above all else, this book is for and about you and your Yeah, Buts.

At any point, my limiting beliefs and those of others could have sabotaged this book completely. At the onset, I didn't know where to start. At many points from then until the very end of the process, I didn't know what to do next, and when I did know, I wasn't always sure I could do it (sound familiar?). Yeah, But… I saw it through. You're at the end of the book, and that's only because I started, despite my Yeah, Buts…

The reason why I started, why I kept going, and why all the people I spoke to and wrote about started and kept going was because we all knew one thing: it wasn't just about us. It was, and is, about all of the people who might benefit if and when we see our plans through. No one will benefit from the book I never wrote. No one will benefit from the business you never built. No one will benefit from the idea you never moved forward.

So, before putting this book down, ask yourself this one fundamental question: Is the potential to make a difference in people's lives worth overcoming my Yeah, Buts for?

> "When you need to change the **how**; just remember your **why**."
>
> - **Wolfe**ism

WHAT'S NEXT?

To keep up to date with resources, share your Yeah, But stories and read the latest stories and updates from *Yeah, But...*, sign up today at www.marcAwolfe.com/YeahButBook

Listen and subscribe to *The Yeah, But Podcast* at https://www.marcawolfe.com/podcast/

Connect with Marc Wolfe by e-mailing him at YeahButMarc@marcAwolfe.com – he will answer your email, no Yeah, buts about it.

Connect with Marc on his social media accounts:

https://www.linkedin.com/in/marcwolfe

https://www.youtube.com/@marcawolfe

ACKNOWLEDGMENTS

This book was a labor of love, and many people played varying roles in helping it move from idea to completion. I am grateful for each one of you. Here are a few (in alphabetical order):

- Ameesha Green
- Bill Rawnsley
- Brenna Wolfe
- Brooks Wolfe
- Christian Ward
- Claire Kelly
- Dayle Savage
- Dick Gygi
- Donna Yurdin
- Emilee Law
- Gemma Rowlands
- Janet Walls
- Katherine Wolfe
- Keri Childers
- Kyle Albuquerque
- Laura Wolfe
- Niall Burgess
- Shaun Hand
- Steve Muscato
- Trey Smith
- Terry Warren

And the *The Yeah, But Podcast* initial guests and interviewees:

- Bonnie Stith
- Brad Wingo
- Brittany Whipple
- Don Baham
- Dr. Ruth Gotian
- Gabrielle Thompson
- Jimmy Ward
- Kevin Dostaler
- Marc Dedman
- Mickey Burnim
- Naomi Kent
- Susie Long

ABOUT THE AUTHOR

Few people can claim to have been kicked out of public school for being "too smart and disruptive," but that's what happened to Marc Wolfe in fourth grade. Ever since that bizarre but pivotal moment, he's known that his life's purpose is to empower others to unlock their potential.

From starting his own photography business at 16 (taking pictures of US Presidents, NFL teams, and other celebrities) through earning a marketing degree while running two businesses (one of which supported and sold early Apple products) to his 25-plus years of working with major companies as an innovation and strategy consultant, Marc's journey has always been guided by principles of service, sharing, and showing people the power they possess.

An International Coaching Federation-certified coach, Marc's continuing mission is to inspire and uplift leaders and audiences through stories, wisdom, and sound advice. He has written articles on leadership for Forbes.com, served as an Inc. 5000 mentor, been hired to work with global companies, and built a reputation for turning conversations into outcomes.

Originally from New Jersey, Marc now lives near Nashville, Tennessee, with his wife and family. *Yeah, But* is his first book and draws on his wealth of experience in listening, seeing, and helping his many accomplished clients.

REFERENCES

1. Everyone that has a life has many different aspects that are part of it, and instead of calling it "work-life balance", I prefer to call it "life agility." You have life and your ability to be agile and flexible is how you include and address each part of your life.

2. A "Wolfeism" is an original quote that Marc A. Wolfe created for his executive coaching and advisory clients and now included in his book, *Yeah, But*. Wolfeisms presents foundational ideas, concepts, or perspectives in an easy-to-remember way.

3. Matt Haber, "Reports: Chinese Democracy Recorded in Many, Many Studios," *Observer,* November 24 2008, https://observer.com/2008/11/reports-ichinese-democracyi-recorded-in-many-many-studios/

4. Jeff Leeds, "The Most Expensive Album Never Made," *The New York Times,* March 6 2005, https://www.nytimes.com/2005/03/06/arts/music/the-most-expensive-album-never-made.html

5. Nicole Sperling, *"Two Veteran C.E.O.s Risk $1.8 Billion on a Streaming App. In a Pandemic."* The New York Times, April 5 2020, https://www.nytimes.com/2020/04/05/business/media/quibi-streaming-app-jeffrey-katzenberg-meg-whitman.html

6. Todd Spangler, "Jeffrey Katzenberg on Quibi's Spectacular Rise and Fall: 'I'm Proud to Own the Failure'," *Variety,* May 23 2023, https://variety.com/2023/digital/news/jeffrey-katzenberg-quibi-proud-to-own-failure-1235623036/

7. Dade Hayes, "Quibi Sells Out $150M In Launch-Year Advertising Inventory," *Deadline,* October 22 2019, https://deadline.com/2019/10/quibi-sells-out-150m-in-launch-year-advertising-inventory-1202766316/

8. Elaine Low, "As Quibi Shutters, So Goes Nearly $2 Billion in Major Hollywood Investments," *Variety,* October 21 2020, https://variety.com/2020/tv/news/quibi-shuts-down-hollywood-investoes-1234812522/

9. Chris Gayomali, "Why Microsoft lost $900 million on the Surface RT," *The Week,* January 8 2015, https://theweek.com/articles/461961/why-microsoft-lost-900-million-surface-rt

10 *History Computer* staff, "The Complete History of Apple Newton," *History Computer,* last updated April 16 2024, https://history-computer.com/technology/the-complete-history-of-apple-newton/

11 Gayomali; Tom Warren, "Apple finally admits Microsoft was right about tablets," *The Verge,* March 19 2020, https://www.theverge.com/2020/3/19/21186500/apple-ipad-pro-vs-surface-pro-trackpad-mouse-inputs-history

12 Rebecca Davis, "The Doctor Who Championed Hand-Washing and Briefly Saved Lives," *NPR,* January 12 2015, https://www.npr.org/sections/health-shots/2015/01/12/375663920/the-doctor-who-championed-hand-washing-and-saved-women-s-lives

13 Biography.com authors, "James Naismith," *Biography.com,* last updated March 26 2021, https://www.biography.com/scholar/james-a-naismith

14 No author given, "Valdez, Alaska Snow & Weather," *Alaska Snowboard Guides,* no date given, https://www.alaskasnowboardguides.com/why-asg/weather-down-days/

15 Jim Park, "How Alaska DOT Uses GPS for Precision Plowing," *Truckinginfo,* April 18 2019, https://www.truckinginfo.com/329914/how-alaska-dot-uses-gps-for-precision-plowing

16 Adam Carlson, "Self-Made Media Mogul: How an Unpaid Intern Became a Barrier-Breaking TV Exec," *People,* December 16 2016, https://people.com/human-interest/nely-galan-tv-producer-telemundo/

17 https://www.goodmorningamerica.com/news/story/suzy-welch-10-10-10-decision-making-process-10270041

18 No author given, "Quotes," *Eisenhower Library,* no date given, https://www.eisenhowerlibrary.gov/eisenhowers/quotes

19 Jay Greene, "The Inside Story of How Microsoft Killed its Courier Tablet," *CNET,* November 1 2011, https://www.cnet.com/tech/tech-industry/the-inside-story-of-how-microsoft-killed-its-courier-tablet/

20 No author given, "Apple Launches iPad," *Apple,* January 27 2010, https://www.apple.com/newsroom/2010/01/27Apple-Launches-iPad/

21 Warren; Nathan Ingraham, "Apple dominates the growing tablet market with 68 percent share, according to IDC," *The Verge,* August 2 2012, https://www.theverge.com/2012/8/2/3215612/apple-tablet-market-domination-q2-2012

22 https://www.windowscentral.com/microsoft-bring-back-courier-2018

23 Stephen Silver, "Ten years ago, Apple's iPhone 3G brought speed and apps to the smartphone," *Apple Insider,* June 8 2018, https://appleinsider.com/articles/18/06/08/ten-years-ago-apples-iphone-3g-brought-speed-and-apps-to-the-smartphone; no author given, "Apple Introduces the New iPhone 3G," *Apple,* June 9 2008, https://www.apple.com/newsroom/2008/06/09Apple-Introduces-the-New-iPhone-3G/

24 https://podcasts.apple.com/us/podcast/the-yeah-but-podcast/id1779330379

25 Amazon staff, "Amazon is delivering at its fastest speeds ever for Prime members in the UK and globally," *Amazon,* July 30 2024, https://www.aboutamazon.co.uk/amazon-fastest-ever-prime-delivery-speed; Matthew Woodward, "Amazon Prime Statistics: Subscribers, Usage & Revenue 2024," *Search Logistics,* updated June 23 2024, https://www.searchlogistics.com/learn/statistics/amazon-prime-statistics/

26 Amelia Lucas, "Olive Garden owner Darden Restaurants buys Ruth's Chris Steak House for $715 million," *CNBC,* May 3 2023, https://www.cnbc.com/2023/05/03/olive-garden-owner-darden-restaurants-buys-ruths-chris-steak-house.html. https://investor.darden.com/news/news-details/2023/Darden-Restaurants-to-Acquire-Ruths-Hospitality-Group-in-715-Million-Transaction/default.aspx

27 No author given, "Ruth Fertel," *Horatio Alger Association of Distinguished Americans,* no date given, https://horatioalger.org/members/detail/ruth-fertel/

28 No author given, "Her life is the stuff of legend," *Way Back Machine Internet Archive,* October 24 2013, https://web.archive.org/web/20131024163101/http://www.fertel.com/images/about_ruth.pdf

29 No author given, "Our Story," *Ruth's Chris Steak House,* no date given, https://m.ruthschris.com/our-story

30 No author given, "Her life is the stuff of legend," *Way Back Machine Internet Archive,* October 24 2013, https://web.archive.org/web/20131024163101/http://www.fertel.com/images/about_ruth.pdf

31 Georgie Barrat, "Six-year-old boy rushed to hospital after Samsung Galaxy Note 7 explodes in his hand," *The Daily Mirror,* September 12 2016, https://www.mirror.co.uk/tech/six-year-old-boy-rushed-8817106

32 Chad Brooks, Sixty-one Percent of Workers are Seeking or Planning to Seek New Jobs," *Business.com,* updated July 21 2023, https://www.business.com/employees/worker-satisfaction-study/

33 No author given, "New Careers for Older Workers," *American Institute for Economic Resarch,* no date given, https://aier.org/new-careers-for-older-workers-2/

34 https://www.cnbc.com/2019/10/31/indeed-nearly-half-of-workers-have-made-a-dramatic-career-switch.html#:~:text=Younger%20professionals%20might%20get%20a,reach%20a%20mid%2Dcareer%20point

35 Douglas Broom, "Having many careers will be the norm, experts say," *World Economic Forum,* May 2 2023, https://www.weforum.org/agenda/2023/05/workers-multiple-careers-jobs-skills/

36 https://www.suzywelch101010.com/ https://www.goodmorningamerica.com/news/story/suzy-welch-10-10-10-decision-making-process-10270041

37 Patrick Kiger, "N. Joseph Woodland: Five Facts About the Bar Code Inventor," *AARP,* December 14 2012, https://blog.aarp.org/legacy/n-joseph-woodland-five-facts-about-the-bar-code-inventor; Gavin Weightman, "The History of the Bar Code," *Smithsonian Magazine,* September 23 2015, https://www.smithsonianmag.com/innovation/history-bar-code-180956704/

38 https://hbr.org/2016/11/why-diverse-teams-are-smarter

39 Louis Dor, "Alan Rickman said this letter changed his life," *Indy100,* January 14 2016, https://www.indy100.com/celebrities/alan-rickman-said-this-letter-changed-his-life-7288641; Maureen Paton, *Alan Rickman: An Unauthorised Biography* (no publisher or date given), https://pdfcoffee.com/alan-rickman-an-unauthorised-biography-pdf-free.html

40 Rosie Walker, "Mini biography", *IMDb,* no date given, https://www.imdb.com/name/nm0000614/bio/

41 No author given, "About," *Susan Boyle Music,* no date given, https://www.susanboylemusic.com/about/

42 No author given, "About Devon Harris," *Devon Harris,* no date given, https://devonharris.com/about-international-motivational-keynote-speaker/

43 No author given, "6 Strategies That Paul Mitchell Used To Turn $300 Into $1.1 Billion," *Beyond,* no date given, https://www.2080.ventures/stories/6-strategies-that-paul-mitchell-used-to-turn-300-into-1-1-billion

44 No author given, "John Paul DeJoria: Doing Good in LA," *Do Good LA*, no date given, https://www.dogoodla.org/john-paul-dejoria

45 Brian Delk, "Even CEOs Have Imposter Syndrome," *Bloomberg*, June 25 2024, https://www.bloomberg.com/news/newsletters/2024-06-25/imposter-syndrome-reported-by-71-of-ceos

46 Michelle Penelope King, "Joy Mangano, The Inspiration Behind The Movie 'Joy,' Shares How To Turn Your Idea Into Dollars," *Forbes*, November 21 2017, https://www.forbes.com/sites/michelleking/2017/11/21/joy-mangano-the-inspiration-behind-the-movie-joy-shares-how-to-turn-your-idea-into-dollars/

47 Luke Ferris, "How Suneera Madhani's Rejected Pitch Led to a Billion-Dollar Startup," *Foundr*, May 13 2024, https://foundr.com/articles/building-a-business/suneera-madhani

48 Anubhav Bhandari, "Is Andre Agassi an Armenian? Everything to Know About His Family's Original Roots," *Essentially Sports*, March 16 2024, https://www.essentiallysports.com/atp-tennis-news-is-andre-agassi-an-armenian-everything-to-know-about-his-familys-original-roots/; Neelabhra Roy, "'I beg him, I tell my father that I don't like being by myself on that huge tennis court': When Andre Agassi was forced to quit soccer for tennis," *Sportskeeda*, modified April 11 2023, https://www.sportskeeda.com/tennis/news-i-beg-him-i-tell-father-i-don-t-like-huge-tennis-court-when-andre-agassi-forced-quit-soccer-tennis

49 No author given, "Biography," *International Tennis Hall of Fame*, no date given, https://www.tennisfame.com/hall-of-famers/inductees/andre-agassi

50 Mark Stevens, "Little tennis for Agassi offspring," *The Courier Mail*, May 16 2011, https://www.couriermail.com.au/ipad/anyone-for-tennis-not-in-the-house-that-andre-agassi-and-steffi-graf-built/news-story/9f2810f1219c58e33dd3791691838720

51 No author given, "Agassi admits use of crystal meth," *BBC Sport*, October 28 2009, http://news.bbc.co.uk/sport1/hi/tennis/8329193.stm; Jenni McKnight, "Brooke Shields discusses failed marriage with very famous ex-husband," *Hello!*, March 22 2024, https://www.hellomagazine.com/brides/516024/brooke-shields-discusses-failed-marriage-andre-agassi/

52 George Anders, "Andre Agassi Struggled In School; Now He Invests In Phonics Startup," *Forbes*, updated January 5 2016, https://www.forbes.com/sites/georgeanders/2016/01/05/andre-agassi-struggled-in-school-now-he-invests-in-phonics-startup/

53 No author given, "Geraldine 'Jerrie' Mock," *National Women's History Museum,* no date given, https://www.womenshistory.org/geraldine-jerrie-mock

54 Various, "American History: Jerrie Mock," *Harmon Museum,* March 19 2019, https://www.womenshistory.org/geraldine-jerrie-mock

55 No author given, "Capt. Shaesta Waiz," *National Air and Space Museum,* no date given, https://airandspace.si.edu/support/wall-of-honor/capt-shaesta-waiz

56 Charlotte Grysolle, "What We Can Learn From James Dyson's 5,126 Failures," *The New York Times,* November 23 2021, https://web.archive.org/web/20240522180454/charlottegrysolle.com/what-we-can-learn-from-james-dysons-5-126-failures/

57 Andrew Dickson, "How we made the Dyson vacuum cleaner," *The Guardian,* May 24 2016, https://www.theguardian.com/culture/2016/may/24/interview-james-dyson-vacuum-cleaner

58 Stephen Dowling, "Frustration and failure fuel Dyson's success," *BBC,* March 14 2013, https://www.bbc.com/future/article/20130312-failure-is-the-best-medicine

59 No author given, "17 Renowned Writer on Overcoming Rejection," *Writing Routines,* no date given, https://www.writingroutines.com/renowned-writers-on-overcoming-rejection.

60 Emily Temple, "The Most-Rejected Books of All Time (Of the Ones That Were Eventually Published)," *Literary Hub,* December 22 2017, https://lithub.com/the-most-rejected-books-of-all-time/

Marc A. Wolfe

At 9 years old, he was removed from public school for being "too smart and disruptive", a moment that shaped his mission to empower others. At 16, he launched a photography business, capturing US Presidents, prominent leaders, and NFL teams. He ran two businesses while earning his marketing degree, including one supporting early Apple products at Fortune 500 companies. With 25+ years as an innovation and strategy consultant, Marc is also an ICF-certified executive coach who's written for Forbes.com and mentored Inc. 5000 companies.